If you can't sell it don't make it

If you can't sell it don't make it

LARRY McMAHON

IRISH MANAGEMENT INSTITUTE
SANDYFORD ROAD
DUBLIN 14

First published in 1978 by the
Irish Management Institute
Sandyford Road
Dublin 14

ISBN 0 903352 14 1

Printed and bound in Ireland
by Mount Salus Press Limited, Dublin.

CONTENTS

INTRODUCTION

If you run your own business, this book is for you. Because your company is still relatively small, you have to work harder than most. Not only are you the managing director – you are also your own production manager, financial manager and marketing manager. This book has been written specifically to help you run you business more effectively.

You can't afford yet to hire a full-time marketing manager. And yet good marketing is the essential ingredient for a successful business. In fact, you could probably say that one reason you're in business for yourself is because you already have an instinctive flair for marketing. As your time is limited, this book will deal only with *useful* aspects of marketing which you can put into practice straight away.

This book is intended as a 'must' for every businessman who is seriously interested in running a successful business. It explains, hopefully in a down-to-earth way, what marketing is all about and how to use it effectively.

I have based the book mainly on my experience with the Irish Management Institute in Dublin, which is Europe's biggest management training centre. At the IMI we run intensive training programmes in marketing for executives from every type of organisation (and from most parts of the world too). They range from the large multinational to the smaller owner-managed firm. In my work I have been struck by the different needs of the owner-manager. In learning terms, he has no time for 'beautiful concepts'. He literally has no time! What he wants are practical techniques which he can use straight away. So I have written the book with this very much in mind.

This book is not intended as just another marketing text-book, nor as a programmed learning text, nor as a cosy fire-side book. In fact, it combines elements from all three types. I call it a guidebook, and hope that you will find it both useful and enjoyable.

Larry McMahon
Irish Management Institute,
Dublin.

How to use this book

One idea behind this book is that you learn about marketing, by *practising* it. By the time you have finished you will have produced a professional marketing plan for one of your own products. If you follow the book properly and carry out the various short exercises, your plan will be on a professional par with any produced by Proctor & Gamble or General Motors!

That sounds like a wild claim, doesn't it? Well, it isn't. Because marketing, as you will shortly learn, is no labyrinth of esoteric techniques. It's just business common-sense, applied in a particular way. You don't have to be a genius to be very good at it. But you do need to keep your eyes open, to think creatively and to work!

It is important that you read the book right through to the end. There is a planned sequence in it. So don't start with chapter 10 and then move to chapter 2! If you do, you'll be lost.

Much of the book deals with pure information – in which case you simply read! But at various stages, we will be concerned with implanting a new attitude or technique. In such cases you will be asked to carry out various short exercises. These exercises will be simple and based on the reality of *your own business.* Please carry out these exercises. This is essential, if you are to obtain the full benefits from this book.

The book contains twelve chapters. A good idea would be to treat it rather like attending a management course. Spread it out over twelve days. Set at least one hour aside each day to read just one chapter. In this way, there will be enough time, between each 'lecture', to allow you to think through the implications of the previous chapter.

CHAPTER ONE

THE BASIC QUESTION

As a concept, the marketing approach is easy enough to understand. The trouble is that it is often difficult to practise. Frequently, firms practise marketing badly because they understand it badly. These first few chapters will take you step-by-step along the right way to think through your marketing problems. You will also be guided to provide your own best solutions to these problems.

WHAT IS MARKETING?

Marketing is essentially a way of looking at your business (some people might call it a 'business philosophy'!). The marketing concept has at its core the notion that business is really about satisfying consumers and *not* about producing a particular product or service. Marketing can be defined in terms of these activities.

1. *Identifying* the needs of a particular group of consumers;
2. *Satisfying* those needs by producing a particular product or service, at the right price;
3. Making optimum *profits* as a result.

The key words in the above definition are *I*dentifying, *S*atisfying and *P*rofits. Let us refer to this approach as the *ISP* approach from now on. It is worth noting that the third activity comes as a result of doing the first two stages well.

Marketing means *ISP.* As mentioned above, it is easy to understand. You might well argue that it is really only applied common-sense. Of course it is! Yet how is it that so many owner/managers practise the *ISP* approach so badly? If we are honest, we must admit that it is often extremely difficult to *I*dentify our consumers. It is also extremely difficult to *S*atisfy them!

Do you suffer from 'Product Fixation'?

Product Fixation is a chronic disease which afflicts both large and small firms. If you are running your own business there is a very good chance that you too suffer from this disease! If you started your business yourself, you probably did so because you felt that you could produce a product or a service. You also believed that your product was as good as, or better than, your competitors'. If you were lucky, you also had evidence that some people would be willing to buy your product.

But your main strength was, in your own mind, your ability to produce the product. After all, it was for that reason that the business was started.

All of this leads to an inevitable fixation on the product (or service) and the technicalities of its production and quality. It is good to have a healthy and businesslike interest in production and product quality. But when it grows too intense it can blot out all concern for the person who is most important to your business – the consumer!

It is not so much the tangible, physical quality (in engineering terms) of your product that matters – but the quality as *seen by your consumer.* There is often a world of difference between how you see your product and how your consumers see it. And it is the consumer's viewpoint which counts in the end. After 'Cash-Flow Amnesia', Product Fixation is the most dangerous disease which can afflict the owner/manager!

The cure for product fixation

Every time you are faced with a marketing problem, or the need to take any decision remotely affecting your consumers, ask yourself the following key question:

–What will this mean through the eyes of my consumer, in terms of benefits to him?

To answer this question honestly, you need to put yourself really in the consumer's shoes. How good are you at doing this? To see things through the eyes of another can be mind-bending for some people. The other man's point-of-view is what matters in marketing – just as in politics.

What happens in the market place?

Figure 1

Let us now take a look at what actually happens in your particular marketplace. How does *ISP* work for you?

Looking at the above illustration, we have four main elements to consider:

1. *You* – the person who decides what product or service your production facility will produce;
2. *Your production facility* – factory, store, hotel, restaurant or agency;
3. *Your product or service* – the thing you put out into the marketplace. It could be a product, or a service such as a

hotel bed-night. From now on let us refer to it as *the product*;

4. *Consumers* – the people who buy and consume your product.

Let us go back to our illustration. You could say that it is a type of communication process between *you* and the *consumers*. And the focal point of this communication is right there in the middle, with the *product*.

In other words:

If some or all of the people on the right-hand side of the illustration happen to decide to buy the product that you happen to produce, then you could have *profitable* communication.

Or look at it from another angle. If you happen to be producing a product which some or all of the people on the right want to buy, then you could have profitable communication.

The trouble is that very often this communication happens more by accident than by design. But if you are serious about marketing you should be managing this situation. You should be making it happen.

Do you owe your present survival in business to the fact that you *managed* this communication process? Or do you owe your survival more to sheer good luck?

How to make things happen your way

In order to communicate with consumers, the first thing to do is to take a closer look at them. You need to ask one fundamental question:

WHO IS MY CONSUMER?

At first glance this appears a rather silly question to ask. It is certainly a simple question, but not silly! In fact, the asking and answering of this particular question is the single most important mental process involved in marketing. Why not try the following exercise for about five minutes.

(1) Take a blank sheet of paper. Then think of any named (branded) consumer product. Do not pick one of your own products! If you are stuck, pick a brand of drink or cigarettes, or perhaps a particular make of car. Then write down the name of the product on the top of the page. And remember, pick one brand – e.g. do not write down 'detergents'. Instead pick OMO or Tide or any particular brand.

(2) Now try to imagine the sort of person who buys this product most often. Think of him/her as one person – the typical heavy buyer of this product.

(3) Write down a description of this 'target consumer'. It should not take more than four or five lines. Use descriptions such as age, social class, married/single, number of children, rural/urban, income level, shopping habits, life style, psychological characteristics, occupation. Use your own terminology to describe him/her (as if you were introducing a character in a novel). Avoid giving a list of different kinds of people who buy the product.

    Instead pick the one group which you think does most of the buying. Then describe that group as one person. Or else pick the common features of each group to re-draw the consumer as one person. When you have finished this pen-portrait, you should have a very clear picture in your mind of the target consumer for this product.

Having completed this exercise, it should be fairly obvious that every marketing decision depends on this description of the target consumer. The product design or formulation must appeal to this person. The price fixed must be the right one for this consumer – not too high and not too low! The pack must be right. It must be distributed so that this particular individual will have an opportunity to buy it. If the product is advertised, it must be done in media which the target consumer reads or sees. Likewise, the message in the advertising must appeal to the particular sort of person you have described.

For example, if you picked one of the more luxurious Mercedes models you would get a very different target consumer than if you picked a Volkswagen beetle. Because the target

consumer is different for each product, the marketing approach must be different also.

The 80/20 rule

In most markets some variation of the 80/20 rule applies. In other words, you often find that 80 per cent of your product sales are accounted for by only 20 per cent of your total potential consumers. What you did in that last exercise was to describe the 20 per cent as one person.

Why one person? Very often firms think of their consumers in terms of statistical categories. The larger firms are more often guilty of this particular sin. Consider the following two market descriptions:

a) 'Housewives, urban, ABC 1 social class, 2 to 4 children, \$10,000–\$12,000 income group, 25 to 35 age bracket.'

b) 'A busy young housewife with three kids. Her husband has an interesting, well-paid job. She has to stay at home to look after the children. She often feels isolated in her surburban home. The house is usually in a state of chaos because of the children. However, when they have visitors, she likes to impress them with her well-kept home and cooking. In these situations, she tries to live up to her husband's position . . .'

Both of the above descriptions refer to the same market. It is far more sensible (and easier too!) to relate to (b) than to (a) in marketing terms. Because you can see the 'busy young housewife' more clearly in your mind's eye, it is easier to think of the type of product design she would go for. It is also easier to 'talk' to her in advertising terms.

It is astonishing that so many owner/managers never ask themselves *'Who is my consumer?'* in a systematic manner.

In the previous exercise you spent five minutes (or maybe ten!) answering this key question for someone else's product. When you get to chapter 4, you will have the opportunity to spend 60 minutes answering this question for one of your own products. As far as your business is concerned, you will hardly ever spend a more profitable 60 minutes!

THE OTHER BASIC QUESTIONS

'Who is my consumer?' is the first basic question to be asked. The others are:

Where is my consumer?
How much does he/she spend?
How often does he buy?
Where does he buy?
Why does he buy?
What exactly is he buying?

You could add many more questions to this list, for your own particular business. At this stage you are asking as many questions as necessary. You want answers which will give you a better fix on the needs of the particular group of consumers you are interested in.

The significance and usefulness of most of the above questions are fairly obvious. However, it is worth spending a little more time considering the last two.

Why does he buy?

Fifty years ago most people bought bread on a regular basis. If you asked anyone at that time why he bought bread, you would get the answer, 'Because I'm hungry'. If you were in the bread business at that time you would be fully aware why people bought your product.

Nowadays, however, many people are buying cake instead – and not just one type of cake, but a wide variety. It is much more difficult to find out why people buy particular types of cakes.

During the early stages of industrialisation in most economies, the vast majority of consumers (that means people!) went to bed hungry. Most people had inadequate clothing, shelter and heating. In other words, their basic physiological (or animal) needs were not satisfied. At that time therefore, most people bought products to satisfy these physiological needs, in order to survive.

These needs are now satisfied for most people in the developed economies. Yet they are buying more than ever. Because the basic needs are satisfied, they are now buying to satisfy other needs. Very often (particularly with consumer products) these needs are emotional and non-rational. And very often these motivations are hidden or sub-conscious.

Take a frank look at your own buying motives. Imagine a market researcher was trying to find out why you buy particular products. You really have three levels of awareness in relation to buying products.

Top level – For some products, you know why you buy them, and you are not ashamed of the reasons. So if a researcher were to ask you, you would be able to give him a reason very easily;

Middle level – With some products, you know why you buy

them, but you will *not* admit the reason to an interviewer. You may tell a white lie or disguise the truth unintentionally. For example, if you buy an expensive car, your real motive might be to impress your business acquaintances and relatives. Yet if asked straight out why you bought it, you would probably start talking about the superb acceleration, bodywork and engineering qualities of the car. What you are doing in this case is covering up your real, emotional motives with rationalisations.

Most of us feel this way when we buy an expensive consumer product such as a car, house or tailor-made suit. The main motives which make us pick a particular product are often emotional, e.g. desire for status. We often feel slight traces of guilt about this. So we rationalise the purchase decision in order to justify it both to ourselves and to others.

Lower level – For some products you are not even consciously aware of your purchase reasons. For example, imagine you are buying a disposable ball-point pen. Your reason for buying a pen may be at the top level of awareness (i.e. you need something to write with). However, when you go into a store you are confronted with, say, five brands. You pick one quickly. If a researcher were to ask you afterwards why you picked that particular brand, what would you say? Probably, 'I liked it', or 'I don't know'. These are not very useful responses to the market researcher.

In this case, there is a real reason, but you are not actively aware of it. It is buried somewhere in your sub-conscious.

'Why does my consumer buy?' is one of the most difficult questions to get an answer to. It is particularly difficult if the reason exists at the middle or lower levels of awareness.

What exactly is my consumer buying?

When one of your consumers buys a product from you, you probably think of it as a valid commercial transaction. And so it is! He parts with his money. In return he gets a tangible product (or service).

But take another look at this transaction – this time from a marketing viewpoint. The consumer parts with his money. In return he gets the tangible product *plus* something else. We call this something else 'consumer satisfaction'. In other words, something happens in your consumer's brain, in return for the cash he has just spent. This mental process could be a feeling or a rational statement to himself.

The tangible product received is still very important. But it is often more realistic to think of your consumers buying a particular consumer satisfaction with their money.

Take a look at this list of products.

Product	*Consumer*	*Consumer satisfaction received*
Insurance	Householder	'Peace-of-mind.'
Pair of shoes	Teenage girl	'Now I really feel I am with the latest fashion trend – just like my friends.'
Office chairs	Purchasing manager	'I was able to save money buying these. They are just as good as more expensive ones. I got a bargain.'
Meal in expensive restaurant	Businessman	'My client will be quietly impressed by my good taste. He can see that I know the right place to eat in this town.'
Air compressor	Committee of engineers in public utility company	'This machine is the most reliable, even though it is fairly expensive. We don't want our equipment to break down. This compressor will give us less trouble.'
Antique painting	Art lover	'This picture will go up in value. It is a very good investment—a hedge against inflation. I can sell it later at a fantastic profit. It's also nice to look at.'

In chapter four you will have an opportunity to spell out the exact consumer satisfaction which *your* product is delivering.

How to get answers to the basic questions

Marketing research is all about getting answers to the basic questions – who?, where?, why?, how much?, etc. Marketing research can cost a lot of money. But it does not have to. Very often either you can do it yourself or dispense with it altogether. Here are the methods for getting the answers you need.

1. *Experience and judgement.* All the years you have spent in your present business must count for something! Think of your brain as a very complex computer. Every event which you have experienced is lodged away somewhere in your brain. The conclusions you drew at the time, together with how this event or observation related to others in your experience – all these data are stored away in your mind. Very often, when confronted with a marketing problem, you 'know' the answer instinctively.

Perhaps you refer to this sense as your 'feel for the market'. What happens in this kind of situation is that your brain deals with the problem subconsciously. Only the solution floats to the conscious surface of your mind. This explains why you often feel so sure about these 'instinctive' decisions.

They are not really instinctive at all. They are the result of your own complex, yet subconscious, problem-solving techniques. Thus your experience-based hunches often produce the right answers.

But be careful! Just as with a computer, the value of the solutions which your brain produces depends on the value of the data which went in originally. Computer specialists say, 'Garbage in, garbage out!', when referring to the value of computerised output.

The way you observe and record data in your brain is crucial. The kinds of values you use in arriving at conclusions are crucial. When arriving instinctively at the answer to one of the basic questions, test it out by asking yourself the following two questions:

–Is your thought-process based on *ISP*?

–Are you really seeing things through the eyes of your consumer?

By doing this, you are bringing *judgement* to bear on your experience-based knowledge.

2. *Observed fact.* This needs no further comment, other than

to say that the closer your contacts with the end-user are, the richer this source will be.

3. *Published statistics.* Every country produces trade statistics of some sort. And this information is free. The larger the country and the more developed its economy, the richer these statistics will be.

The types of organisations who publish useful material are: government statistics offices (who should at least keep records of imports and exports); export promotion boards; government ministries; trade associations; chambers of commerce; trade magazines; and business research agencies.

The problem with free published statistics is that you have to dig to find what you want. Here are some suggestions.

Try your local library. Or better still, if there is a business or trade library convenient, try that. Ask the librarian for help with your information problem. Most librarians are only too glad to assist. If they have not got the publication or information you need, they will at least tell you where you can get it.

Go out and ask people. Make a nuisance of yourself if necessary! Use your telephone. Write letters. Call in person. If some official in a government agency can help you, then it is up to you to make sure that you get that help. If the data you want are buried somewhere in a large bureaucratic organisation, it is very important to strike up a good relationship with one of the officials.

More often than not, you will be surprised at how anxious to help most people are. This is particularly true, when you are dealing with an agency such as a government export promotion board.

4. *Your own internal records.* If you are selling directly to the final consumer, do you keep records of all the people you sell to? These can be a very useful source of information. It may be possible to really pinpoint your typical heavy-buying consumer and where typically he comes from.

5. *Systematic market observation.* This is probably something you do anyway as a matter of routine. It is particularly important when you are either starting your business, or launching a new product. Sample your competitors' products. Talk to their consumers. Generally, observe as much as you can. Trade fairs are very useful in this context.

6. *Syndicated market surveys.* Many market research agencies carry out regular surveys of a particular market. What happens is that they send out their teams of interviewers with a questionnaire on a regular basis. Or else the interviewers record market development, e.g. sales levels, stock levels and display facings. The research company then sells this information to the suppliers in the market. If one of these regular surveys is carried out in your market, it may provide a way of getting information at a very low price. For instance you could, for a fee, have a special question of your own added to the questionnaire. These syndicated surveys are often referred to as audits or omnibus surveys.

7. *Marketing research.* If you have tried the approaches 1 to 6 above, but still feel you need more information, then you should have a talk with one or two market research agencies. Remember that formal research need not cost a fortune. Owner/managers of smaller firms often avoid market research in the belief that it is a luxury which only the Unilevers or the IBMs can afford. This is not true.

One word of warning! Beware of any attempts made to overawe you with statistical research jargon. Remember that what you need are answers to specific *basic questions.* Discuss these with the company. Usually, they will help you to clarify exactly what you need, and how useful these data might be to you.

After your meeting, prepare a written brief for them outlining your needs, and mentioning your cost limitations. Invite them to submit a proposal to you. This proposal should describe the information you will receive, the research methodology and questionnaire, and the cost. You then decide whether or not to go ahead, on the basis of whether or not the information would justify the expense, in your opinion.

Another useful approach would be to contact the marketing professor or lecturer in your local university, technical college or business school. He might well be interested in doing your research for you on a private basis. The idea here is that he would design the survey and use his students to do the field research work for a nominal fee. Many business school marketing lecturers are anxious to do this kind of work. The advantages to them are – money, practical business experience for the students and closer contact with the local business community.

How far are we now?

Having read this first chapter, including the five-minute exercise, you should have a complete idea of what the first stage of marketing is all about. Going back to the *ISP* model, you now understand what is meant by *identifying the needs of a particular group of consumers.* Essentially, this vital stage of marketing is about asking and answering the basic questions.

In the next chapter, we will consider the second stage of marketing – *satisfying those needs.* In other words, if we know the answers to the basic questions, what should we actually *do* about it in the market-place?

CHAPTER TWO

SATISFYING THOSE NEEDS

In the previous chapter we considered the *satisfaction* which your consumers are buying in the market. Now let us consider what you are offering. In other words, what is your consumer responding to, which *he* thinks will deliver this satisfaction?

He is responding to the actual product. He is also responding to its price, the way it is promoted and where it is made available to him. In other words, he is responding to a *mix* of elements – and not just the product itself.

The illustration in the previous chapter should now be redrawn as follows:–

Figure 2

Having answered the Basic Questions, let us imagine that we have identified our consumers (the ones with the shaded faces!).

These are the people we want to go for. We are *not* aiming at the total group of consumers. We are aiming at one specific segment. This brings up a very important marketing rule:

DON'T BE GREEDY!

It is folly to try to be all things to all men. You may sometimes find yourself seduced by the notion that your product will appeal to every consumer in your market. This is a fanciful delusion. It is far better to aim your mix at one very specific segment of your total market. And then hit them hard with your total mix.

For example, think of this book you are reading, as a product. When planning this book it was tempting to produce a marketing textbook which would appeal to chief executives of large firms, marketing managers, non-marketing directors and managers, owner/managers running their own companies and students of business administration. But if such a book had been written it would have satisfied nobody. Students would have rejected it as not academic enough. Marketing managers would have rejected it for its lack of 'big company marketing' flavour. And the owner/manager (i.e. you) would have rejected it as not practical or helpful for your particular situation.

It was finally decided to aim this product at one segment – the owner/manager. When picking which segment to aim at, one looks at the following criteria:

1. competitive activity aimed at each segment;
2. how likely is each segment to purchase such a product;
3. how much will it cost to sell to each segment?;
4. production capability;
5. your relative ability to produce a product at the right price to satisfy each segment;
6. which segment is likely to generate most profit for you? (in other words, the last part of the *ISP* approach).

Having considered the above criteria, it was decided to aim this book at the owner/manager. The fact that *you* are now reading the book proves the point! It pays not to be too greedy.

THE MARKETING MIX

Satisfying consumer needs really means producing the right marketing mix for each of your products. Once the basic questions have been answered, this is the second major task. The first stage is information-gathering. The second stage is doing something about it.

The marketing mix really means everything you do about your product in the market-place which affects your consumers in any way. One useful way of thinking of this mix is in terms of *'the four Ps'* – choosing the right *product, place, promotion* and *price.*

If any one element in your mix is wrong, your target consumer will not buy. For instance, if your price is too high, they may reject it as being too expensive. Or if the price is too low they may also reject it. They may feel that at such a low price, the product's quality would not be high enough for them. Or (if it is a consumer product) they might not wish to be seen buying such a 'cheap' product.

Every product you sell has its own marketing-mix. What the mix looks like is your responsibility. You may sometimes think of your market as a vague, fluctuating, unpredictable and dynamic force, which may or may not move your way. You may feel that whatever happens in the market is somehow outside your control.

There is some truth in this. However, you do have almost complete control in at least one area – the marketing-mix for your product. You dictate what happens in this area. For the rest of the market, you have the answers to your basic questions to guide you.

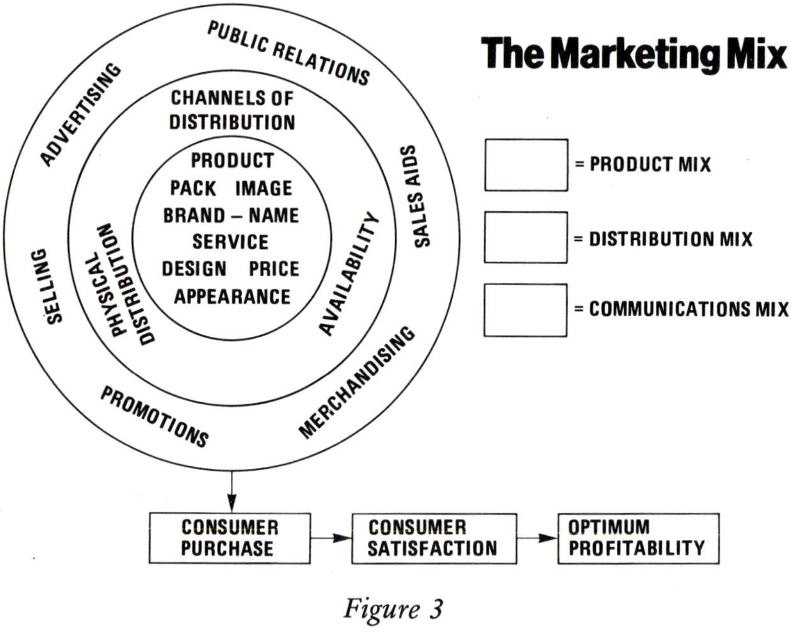

Figure 3

Think of the marketing-mix for any one of your products in terms of the illustration in Figure 3. Imagine that everything within the three concentric circles represents your mix. You will notice that the total mix is divided into three sub-mixes.

The product mix: This includes all those elements which are most closely associated with the product itself. You will probably find that the elements within this circle are the most important for any one of your products. Despite all the emphasis placed on sales techniques and advertising nowadays, the product itself is still the most important element. Generally you think long and hard, before deciding to change one of the elements within this inner circle. The effects of changing an element in the product mix are usually more dramatic and irrevocable, than changing an element in one of the outer circles.

The distribution mix: What this means is everything you do to move your product from your warehouse to the final consumption point.

What combination of wholesalers, retailers and door-to-door distribution is right for this product (i.e. channels of distribution)? Should you use your own transport fleet or an outside carrier (i.e. physical distribution)? How widely *available* should your product be?

The communications mix: This includes all the elements you use in order to tell people about your product and persuade them to buy. How should you convince a particular group of people that your product is the one which best suits its needs?

Using the marketing mix

Marketing is not just a fancy word for selling. Selling is only part of your total marketing effort. Likewise, advertising is only part of marketing.

How important should each element be within the marketing-mix for one of your products? This depends on factors such as the type of product, the nature of your market, competitive activity, your sales targets and the money you can afford to spend. For instance, which of the two elements, advertising or direct selling, should you spend more money on? If you look at Figure 4 below, you will see some critical factors which would tend to move you in one direction or the other.

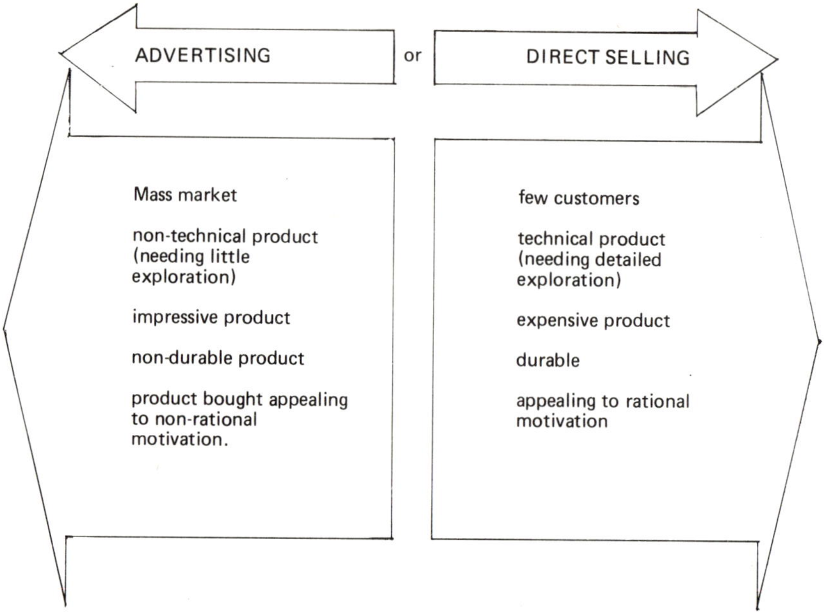

Figure 4

For some products, you might decide to concentrate all your efforts on either advertising or selling. In other cases, you might decide on a combination of both. For example, imagine you were selling a low-priced novelty food product through supermarkets (e.g. children's confectionery). In this case you would probably concentrate on advertising only to the final consumer (children). However, you also have to move this product through supermarkets. You should persuade the store manager to stock and display the item. If you look back at Figure 4 above, it is obvious that you would be better to sell to him rather than advertise. Thus you would sell to the store manager (to push the product into the right distribution channel) and advertise to the consumer (to pull the product through).

As mentioned earlier, getting the right marketing mix is the main action part of marketing. This is the *S* of *ISP.* It is usually impossible to know exactly whether or not you have the optimal mix. And this is true for even the most sophisticated multinational marketing concerns. The irony is that you still have to try working towards an optimal mix, which you cannot actually visualise!

In an on-going situation, you review your marketing and profit achievements for the previous year. Then you ask yourself, 'Could I have done better? Is there a weak element in my mix? Did I get the balance wrong between elements? How can I improve each element in the mix?'. You then take another look at the answers to your Basic Questions. You then decide to change (and hopefully improve) some elements in your mix. All the time, you are gradually improving the mix from year to year—and working towards an optimal mix. It is essentially a trial and error process. The way to reduce errors is to spend more time on the Basic Questions.

Formulating the marketing-mix is most difficult when you are launching a completely new product. In this case you have little previous experience to go on. Because you are taking such a big risk, the more information you have the better. Again, even more time and money should be spent on getting answers to the Basic Questions beforehand.

The marketing-mix you arrive at depends on the answers you get to the Basic Questions. In many cases, arriving at the appropriate mix follows automatically from these answers. Take another look at the exercise you did in chapter 1. Then look at Figure 3 above (see page 26). You should find that the general nature of the appropriate marketing-mix is dictated to a large extent by the answers you gave to only one basic question: 'Who is my consumer?'.

The managing director of an Irish textile firm investigated the United States market a few years ago. He spent no money on formal market research. But he did at least ask himself the basic questions. The answers he got virtually told him how every element in the mix should be, with one exception. The exception in this case was distribution. He could not get enough information on this element. So he took a risk on one of his distribution options—and it worked. His eventual success in the U.S. market was due to the fact the he cut down on risks. Instead of taking risks on every element in his mix, he used the basic questions, and only had to take a big risk on distribution.

In the chapter after next (chapter 4) you will be able to work through both the basic questions and the ideal marketing-mix, for one of your own products.

CHAPTER THREE

INDUSTRIAL MARKET OR CONSUMER MARKET?

Think about the people who buy your main product. They will fall into one of two broad categories. They are part of either a consumer market or an industrial market. In other words—your product is sold to a *consumer market* if it is bought in the end by a consumer for his own personal satisfaction (or that of his family).

Your main product, however, may not be bought in the end by a personal consumer. It may be bought by another company. This (customer) company then uses your product to help it to produce whatever it produces. In this case you are in an *industrial market.* Examples of industrial market products would be: machinery and equipment, raw-materials, fabricated materials, component parts, research goods, operating supplies and some services.

The 'modern' approach to marketing was started back in the early 'fifties by some of the larger consumer-product multinationals. As a result, many businessmen think that marketing only applies if you're selling detergents or cornflakes. Not so! The same *ISP* approach applies whether you're selling margarine or heavy machinery. Only the details and emphasis change.

For the rest of this chapter we will be looking at some of the peculiarities of industrial product marketing. If you are a consumer product man, then you may prefer to skip the rest of this chapter, and move on to chapter 4. But stay with me, industrial marketers!

The first thing to remember about any industrial market is that there is no inherent demand. In other words, nobody is buying your product just for the fun of it! The demand for your type of industrial product depends almost totally on the demand for your customers' products. The demand for their products again depends ultimately on a consumer market somewhere down the line.

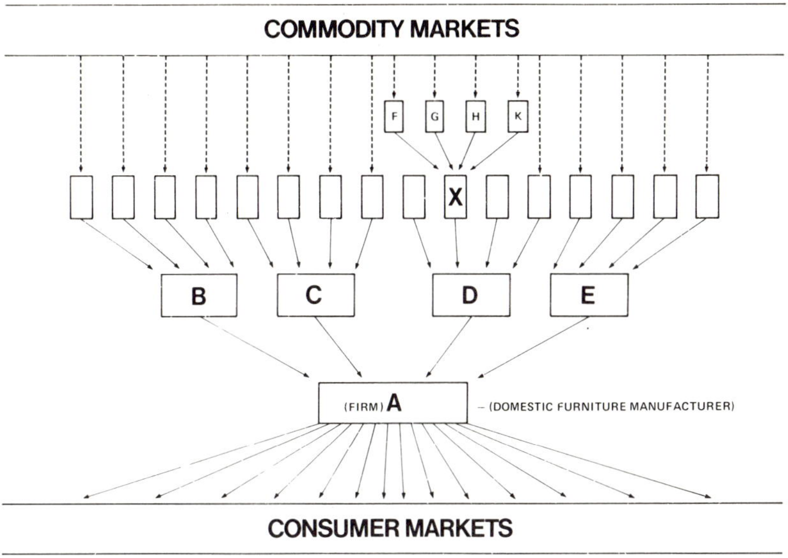

Figure 5

Take a look at Figure 5. No, it's not the interior of a transistor radio! It's quite simple–like all marketing ideas. Let us take any consumer-product company. In this case it is 'A', a manufacturer of domestic furniture. 'A' sells direct to consumers. The sales of A's product depend directly on the demand from the consumer market.

But to carry on his business, A needs to buy in certain products. Let us imagine he has four suppliers: B (wood); C (metal attachments, screws, etc.); D (plastic handles) and E (upholstery material). (In fact A would have much more than four suppliers–but let's keep it simple!)

B, C, D and E also have their suppliers, who in turn have theirs, who in turn have theirs . . . . right back to the suppliers of commodity products, such as oil, metal ores and agricultural products.

Where do *you* come into all of this? Let us again imagine that you are in there as 'X'. You have four suppliers (F, G, H and K). You produce metal moulds. You sell these to D (the plastic handle manufacturer).

In fact, of course, you would also sell to other customers. But again let's keep it simple and imagine you sell only to D. The demand for your metal moulds depends on the demand for plastic furniture handles–which in turn depends on the demand for domestic furniture.

This is what we mean when we say that the demand for any industrial product is *derived* ultimately from consumer demand.

If we had enough space, the diagram in Figure 5 would look like an upside-down pyramid–all depending on 'A'. In reality A is not the only company selling consumer products. There are more upside-down pyramids! A picture of the total economy would look like Figure 6 below.

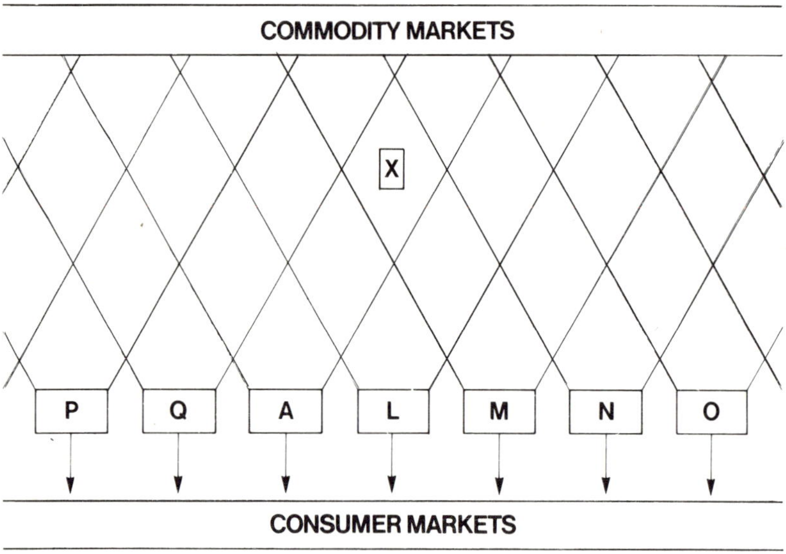

Figure 6

Firm X now belongs to three triangles. It supplies firm A, L and M.

The problem for the industrial marketer is that he has relatively little influence on the ultimate, consumer markets–even though he ultimately depends on them. If A sells less furniture, there is very little that X can do about it. What X (that means you!) must do, however, is sell more to L and M. You must also find other customers (not necessarily furniture manufacturers) who could use your metal moulds.

You have probably noticed how the total demand in your market fluctuates widely from year to year. *Fluctuating demand* is another feature of industrial markets. To understand why this happens, take another look back at Figure 5 (page 31).

Let us say that the demand for domestic furniture drops by three per cent in any given year. In order to maintain his profitability A will economise on bought-in materials. He will reduce inventory levels. If he regularly replaces one machine each year, this year he makes do with what he has. The result might be that the money value of D's sales to A will drop by six per cent and your sales (X) to D will drop perhaps by 10 per cent!

The reverse will tend to happen when A's sales go up by three per cent.

If we move to Figure 6 we can extend this idea to the total economy. If the total level of consumer demand drops you get a 'multiplier-effect' working back through the economy. The further back your firm is from the end-consumer, the more dramatic will be the drop in demand for your product. This is why producers of commodity products experience such wide fluctuations. The farmer is a typical example. If demand for beef increases by 30 per cent one year, he will sell all he can and invest heavily in beef production. But next year beef demand may drop 40 per cent and mutton may increase dramatically!

This situation has a lot to do with the psychology of businessmen. If a recession begins, it feeds on itself, as pessimism spreads. Conversely, in boom times, optimism runs riot.

The individual industrial marketer looks at his total market as a cake. He expects to get a certain slice. The trouble is that the cake itself may increase or decrease very rapidly. He has to be that much more adaptable than the consumer marketer.

During boom times he must invest in marketing activity to increase his share of the cake (while hopefully his competitors are just sitting back letting it all happen!). During recessions he can often only survive by getting a bigger share of the shrinking cake. He needs marketing more than ever during hard times.

Another problem is that your customer is not a housewife. Your customer is a firm—an organisation. So who exactly are you selling to? You can identify a customer-firm easily enough. But the real problem is which individual (or individuals) must you sell to? Is there a key decision-maker?

More often than not there are a number of people, within your customer firm, who influence whether or not your product is bought. Let us say you are an office equipment distributor. Within any of your customer firms you will find an office manager. Then there are the people who would actually use your product —clerks and typists. The firm's purchasing manager will also have a say. Even the receptionist will influence the purchasing decision —she may not let your salesman in! What we are talking about here is the idea of the *buying centre*—the group of people within the firm who influence (directly or indirectly) the purchasing decision.

You (or your salesman) need to find out the nature of the buying centre in each of your customer firms. You may need to sell to a number of people in turn, and at different levels. Or perhaps there is really only one key influencer. In this case, make sure you sell to him and not someone else. It is worth pointing out that the key influencer may be quite low down in the organisation. The chief executive is not necessarily interested in which brand of note-paper the company buys!

Another important feature is that industrial buyers are usually rational—unlike end consumers. You (as a consumer) will buy a new car largely for irrational emotional reasons. You buy a nice warm feeling of comfort and prestige. If you were rational about it, you would buy a much cheaper model and think mainly of economy and the function of moving you and your family from A to B.

Industrial buyers (as I say) are usually rational. But not always 100 per cent rational. Say (as often happens) a buyer is faced with a choice of buying one brand out of three possible and near-identical brands. When he decides on one brand, he will be influenced by irrational factors such as the 'personality' (brand-image) of each brand, his relationship with the three salesmen and inertia (i.e. laziness).

But as your customers are nearly always rational, you must give them rational reasons for buying.

In industrial marketing you also get the phenomena of *order-splitting* and *reciprocity*. Both of these are two-edged swords. With order-splitting many customers prefer to buy from more than one supplier. It reduces their dependence on one source. They can also play the old game of setting off one supplier against the other.

Reciprocity occurs usually when your customer's firm is part of a conglomerate. He says: 'I'll buy from you—but you in turn must buy your supplies from one of our associate companies!'.

To sum up then, the main distinguishing features of industrial product marketing are:

- Derived demand;
- Widely fluctuating demand;
- The buying centre;
- Mainly rational buying motives;
- Order splitting;
- Reciprocity.

As mentioned earlier, despite the differences between consumer and industrial marketing, the game is still basically the same. The same *ISP* approach applies.

In the next chapter we (you and I together) will try to make *ISP* work for you in your market.

CHAPTER FOUR

A "DO-IT-YOURSELF" MARKETING KIT (PART 1)

We now come to the key chapter of this book. It's the key chapter because this is where *you* put in some work. It will take no more than sixty minutes to work through it. But I can guarantee that you will rarely have spent an hour more profitably for your business.

Basically the chapter consists of a few simple exercises. The idea is to take you through the ISP approach in a way which is real for your business. ISP is merely a simple business philosophy. And the best way to learn any philosophy is to practise it—if only for an hour.

Having done it once, it will be easy to repeat for other marketing situations. After a little further practice of the ISP approach, it should become second nature. And that's when you get the real pay-off.

Preliminary

Pick one product (or service) which you currently sell. Preferably pick a product with which you reckon you have a marketing problem. It might be your most important profit-earner or a relatively new product which hasn't really taken off yet.

Alternatively, pick a new product which you are thinking of producing. Another possibility would be to pick a product which you already sell in your local home market but are now thinking of launching in a new market (perhaps in a foreign country).

Write down the name and/or description of this product (or service) below:

Product Name . . . .

Product Description . . . .

. . . .

. . . .

EXERCISE 1

Who is my consumer?

This is a bit like the exercise you did in the first chapter. Only this time it's for one of your own products.

Remember the 80/20 rule! Describe the consumer who is most important for you. Describe him (or her) as one person. Use descriptions such as age, income level, sex, married or single, shopping habits, position, family involvement, number of children, social class, life-style, psychological make-up, rural/urban, state of mind, etc. What you do is draw a pen-portrait of the typical heavy-buying consumer you're after. In effect you take all the main common characteristics of your consumers. Then join them together to describe a 'typical' representative consumer. Describe him *as one person.* You end up describing a sort of Frankenstein!

This description should be no longer than a couple of paragraphs. It's rather like introducing a new character in a novel.

If you are marketing an industrial product you do much the same thing. However, instead of thinking of an individual consumer initially, you describe the typical, heavy-buying customer-firm. Then you describe the typical key decision-maker in the firm as your target consumer. If the idea of the buying centre applies, then you need to describe the other people who will have a say in the purchasing decision.

Now have a go! All you need is a pen. The next few blank pages are all yours!

Now, having described your target consumer, here is a little test to determine how well you've done it. Having described him, can you see him clearly enough in your mind's eye to actually write him a personal letter? If you can, well done! If you can't, then go back again and have another go until you really can see him clearly.

EXERCISE 2

Where is my consumer?

After the last exercise, this one should be easy! Where are most of your consumers (existing and potential) located, in geographic terms? What else can you say about their location? Are they in high-rise apartment blocks or suburban sprawls? If you already keep records of your existing customers, why not analyse these data. Maybe it will give you a clearer picture.

Now write down what you can in the blank spaces below. Why write it down? This will become clearer to you later. At this stage you have to take my word for it that the sheer discipline of writing things down produces clearer thinking.

EXERCISE 3

What else can I say about him?

In this exercise you throw in as much additional information as you can about your target consumer—and you *write it down*. Some of this information may not seem very useful to you at this stage. But write it down anyway—you never know in the marketing game! It can often happen that you get that vital advantage over your competitors, simply by using one odd piece of information which nobody thought of before.

To guide you with this exercise, here is a list of thought-provoking questions:

– How much does he spend?
– How often does he buy?
– Where does he buy?
– How does he buy?
– What other brands does he buy?
– Why does he buy?

Just add any other basic questions, that you can think of, to this list. Then fill up the following blank pages.

EXERCISE 4

What 'Bundle of Satisfactions' does he buy (when he buys my product)?

Some people buy your product. Other people buy your competitor's products. So why on earth should some people buy yours? Can you think of one good reason? If *you* can't, how can you expect *them* to?

Remember most consumers buy for a reason. It may not always be a 'rational' reason. The reason may even be subconscious in some cases. But there is a reason. To be successful in marketing you must have a very good fix on this reason.

In the previous exercise, you had a go at telling yourself 'why' your consumer buys. You probably came up with a fairly general 'why'. In this exercise you will refine and clarify this further.

You have already described your target consumer as fully as possible. Now be honest. Not everybody who fits this description buys your product. Some people, who fit the description perfectly, buy your competitors' product. In this exercise, I want you to focus on the target consumer, who actually does buy your product.

Imagine him at the moment of purchase . . . . He pays out his money (or signs the order) . . . . In return he gets your product. But he also gets something else. In his mind, he also receives a 'Bundle of Satisfactions'. This 'Bundle of Satisfactions' is what he really buys. It's much more important than the actual product itself—from a *marketing* point of view.

The best way to get a fix on this 'Bundle of Satisfactions' is to imagine your consumer as if he were talking to himself at the moment of purchase. Now in reality your consumer very often doesn't talk to himself in this situation. Perhaps he merely grunts mentally, at a *conscious* level. But that doesn't matter. The point is that in order to get at this 'Bundle of Satisfactions' (which may or may not be subconscious) you have to ask yourself: 'If my consumer were talking to himself at the moment of purchase, what would he say?' Then you simply write it down. The statement would consist of one or more sentences. Always enclose the statement in inverted commas.

When you have it written down, then you know *exactly* what your consumer buys. In order to get this done right, you really need to project yourself into the mind of the consumer. Try it now for a few minutes. Remember *you are the consumer at the moment of purchase.*

What are you saying to yourself? . . . .

"

"

Well done! You may think that what you've just written is a pretty harmless statement. But, believe me, it's not. Getting the 'Bundle of Satisfactions' right is the *key* to marketing success.

EXERCISE 5

What 'Bundle of Satisfactions' are your competitors selling?

Now do the same again for the main competitive products in your market. By competitive products, I mean similar products to yours which are bought by at least some of your target consumers. Again, imagine you are the consumer in each case—and talk to yourself at the moment of purchase. You will find a number of blank pages following this. Allow one page for each of your main competitors.

Competitive Product No. 1

Product Name: . . . .

Bundle of Satisfactions

"

"

Competitive Product No. 2

Product Name: . . . .

Bundle of Satisfactions

"

"

Competitive Product No. 3

Product Name: ....

Bundle of Satisfactions

"

"

Competitive Product No. 4

Product Name: . . . .

Bundle of Satisfactions

"

"

Again, well done! As you probably noticed, some competitors are aiming a different bundle of satisfactions at *your* consumer. Others are aiming at a different consumer altogether.

You should now have a list of competitive bundles. Each one (including your own) should be different (if only slightly) from the others. This helps you now to get a real fix on your consumer. What then is special about your consumer? He is exactly as described by you in exercises 1 to 3. *And* he buys the particular bundle of satisfactions described in exercise 4. That's what he is looking for in the market-place. That's what's special about him.

If it happens that you find that your bundle is really the same as one or more of your competitors, you have a special problem. Yours is a parity product. But more about that in the next chapter.

You have now completed the first part of the ISP approach—the *Information* bit. As mentioned earlier, this part of marketing is the most important part. You may feel you have merely asked yourself a few simple basic questions. Exactly! You have done just that. And you have written down the answers.

You may feel that you haven't really done anything yet. You certainly haven't yet made anything happen in the market-place. But you will! The point is that you now have the right information on which to base your marketing decisions!

The reason so much marketing effort is wasted is that so many businessmen do not ask these basic questions beforehand. They feel they must *do* something immediately. So they rush blindly ahead—redesigning their product, introducing new advertising and packaging and cutting their prices. There is simply no use in doing anything in to-day's competitive market-place without asking these basic questions first.

Think about it! You spent about sixty minutes on this chapter. And you wrote down your answers. You *already* have a distinct advantage over your competitors. You have more information. You know more about the market than they do. You even know more about why consumers buy *their* products!

Having put in this amount of effort, you will find it easier to make your marketing decisions. In fact, many of your marketing-action decisions will be almost automatic. One thing is certain.

The odds are now much more in favour of your making the *correct* decisions about marketing action.

The next chapter will help you further in making these decisions.

CHAPTER FIVE

A "DO-IT-YOURSELF" MARKETING KIT (PART II)

You have completed the 'I' part of ISP. It is now time to turn to the 'S'—how to satisfy those needs. As mentioned earlier, we satisfy the needs of our consumer by providing him with the right *marketing-mix.*

You already know who he is, and what his needs are. He is looking for the *'Bundle of Satisfactions'* already identified by you.

What happens in practise is that your consumer looks around in the marketplace. He takes a look at each marketing-mix presented to him. He then *relates to that mix which he thinks will best deliver the 'bundle of satisfactions' he needs.*

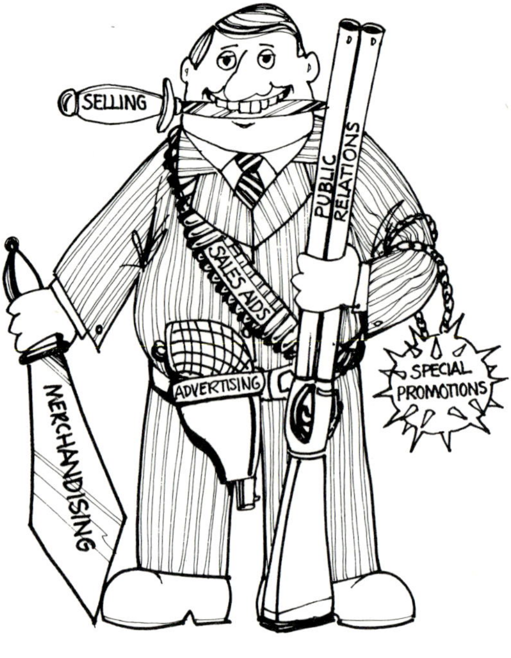

So your job now is to make sure that *your* marketing-mix delivers this 'bundle' better than any of your competitors.

But before you start changing anything, take a look at the marketing-mixes actually on offer at the moment. Three simple exercises follow which will help you to do this in a systematic way.

EXERCISE 6

Marketing-mix description for my product.

On the following pages, simply describe the marketing-mix for your product. Then describe the mixes for your competitors' products. Pick only those products most directly competitive with your own. That means products which are bought by consumers similar to your target consumer (as described by you in chapter 4).

You have already described the 'bundles-of-satisfaction' offered by each product, in the previous chapter. What you do now is describe the marketing-mix in each case.

It is important to describe each marketing-mix as much as possible in terms of what each element means to the consumer!

It is worth mentioning also that the single most important element in any marketing-mix is usually the *product* itself.

(a) The Product Mix

How does the consumer see the product itself, in terms of product features, performance, design, brand-name, formulation, appearance, back-up service, packaging, price, and credit terms?

___

___

(b) The Distribution Mix

How does the product arrive in the consumer's possession? How is it physically distributed to him? What channels (e.g. wholesalers, retailers, etc.) are used? How widely available is it to consumers? How can they get it? How soon is it delivered?

(c) The Communications Mix

How is the consumer persuaded to buy the product? How much, and what sort of selling is used? How often (if at all) does the consumer get a sales call? How is the product advertised? What does the advertising say to the consumer? What public relations, merchandising, promotions and sales aids are used to persuade the consumer? Are different methods of persuasion used at different stages of distribution?

Now you do the same again for each main competitive product on the following pages.

Marketing Mix Description for . . . . (Product Name)

(d) The Product Mix

How does the consumer see the product itself, in terms of product features, performance, design, brand-name, formulation, appearance, back-up service, packaging, price, and credit terms?

(e) The Distribution Mix

How does the product arrive in the consumer's possession? How is it physically distributed to him? What channels (e.g. wholesalers, retailers, etc.) are used? How widely available is it to consumers? How can they get it? How soon is it delivered?

(f) The Communications Mix

How is the consumer persuaded to buy the product? How much, and what sort of selling is used? How often (if at all) does the consumer get a sales call? How is the product advertised? What does the advertising say to the consumer? What public relations, merchandising, promotions and sales aids are used to persuade the consumer? Are different methods of persuasion used at different stages of distribution?

Marketing Mix Description for . . . . (Product Name)

(d) The Product Mix

How does the consumer see the product itself, in terms of product features, performance, design, brand-name, formulation, appearance, back-up service, packaging, price, and credit terms?

(e) The Distribution Mix

How does the product arrive in the consumer's possession? How is it physically distributed to him? What channels (e.g. wholesalers, retailers, etc.) are used? How widely available is it to consumers? How can they get it? How soon is it delivered?

(f) The Communications Mix

How is the consumer persuaded to buy the product? How much, and what sort of selling is used? How often (if at all) does the consumer get a sales call? How is the product advertised? What does the advertising say to the consumer? What public relations, merchandising, promotions and sales aids are used to persuade the consumer? Are different methods of persuasion used at different stages of distribution?

Marketing Mix Description for . . . . (Product Name)

(d) The Product Mix

How does the consumer see the product itself, in terms of product features, performance, design, brand-name, formulation, appearance, back-up service, packaging, price, and credit terms?

(e) The Distribution Mix

How does the product arrive in the consumer's possession? How is it physically distributed to him? What channels (e.g. wholesalers, retailers, etc.) are used? How widely available is it to consumers? How can they get it? How soon is it delivered?

(f) The Communications Mix

How is the consumer persuaded to buy the product? How much, and what sort of selling is used? How often (if at all) does the consumer get a sales call? How is the product advertised? What does the advertising say to the consumer? What public relations, merchandising, promotions and sales aids are used to persuade the consumer? Are different methods of persuasion used at different stages of distribution?

Marketing Mix Description for . . . . (Product Name)

(d) The Product Mix

How does the consumer see the product itself, in terms of product features, performance, design, brand-name, formulation, appearance, back-up service, packaging, price, and credit terms?

(e) The Distribution Mix

How does the product arrive in the consumer's possession? How is it physically distributed to him? What channels (e.g. wholesalers, retailers, etc.) are used? How widely available is it to consumers? How can they get it? How soon is it delivered?

(f) The Communications Mix

How is the consumer persuaded to buy the product? How much, and what sort of selling is used? How often (if at all) does the consumer get a sales call? How is the product advertised? What does the advertising say to the consumer? What public relations, merchandising, promotions and sales aids are used to persuade the consumer? Are different methods of persuasion used at different stages of distribution?

EXERCISE 7

What should my marketing-mix be in the future?

We now come to the *action* bit at last. Call it 'marketing strategy' if you like. What we are really getting at is this:

> In the light of what you now know about your target consumer, the 'bundle-of-satisfactions' he gets from your product and your competitors', your marketing-mix and your competitors', ... *what should you do?*

Remember, only you can ultimately make these strategic decisions. No business consultant, market researcher, advertising agency or marketing guide-book can do it for you!

What you can say now is that (providing you worked at the previous exercises) you have the correct information on which to base your decisions.

A few more thought-provoking questions are provided in this exercise—to help you towards these decisions.

(a) Think about your *target consumer* and the 'bundle-of-satisfactions' he ought to get when he buys your product.

Can you improve your marketing-mix so that it better delivers this bundle? If so, how? How can you improve each element in your mix—and thus *improve this product's profitability?* Consider all the possibilities you can with each element. With some elements, of course, you will find that what you're currently doing is probably just right.

Write down each element below and how you should change it. Refer back to what you've already written in Exercise 6 (a), (b) and (c) as necessary.

(a) ____

____

____

____

____

____

____

____

____

____

____

(b) Of all the bundles offered to your target consumer (by you and your competitors) which bundle has the greatest potential? In other words, is one bundle more popular—and is it likely to grow in popularity?

If your product is already delivering this bundle, congratulations! Then move on to the next page.

If not, however, you need to think seriously about your product. Perhaps it offers a new bundle which no other product is yet delivering. Why not get in first with it?

Maybe one of your competitors is already delivering this 'growth' bundle more than adequately. Can you take him on? Should you try? Have you got the technical and marketing know-how to produce a superior marketing-mix? Remember, if you do take him on directly, *your* mix must be noticeably more attractive to the consumer. Otherwise you end up with a 'me-too' product. Why should *his* consumer buy your mix—unless it is better?

Just write down any general thoughts you have on this, below:

(c) It is quite likely that the bundle your product delivers is similar to some of your competitor's products. It is also quite likely that your existing marketing-mix is similar. In other words, it is quite likely that, right now, yours is a *parity* product, or a 'me-too' product.

In this situation, you can only improve your profitability if your marketing-mix is noticeably and outstandingly *better* than your competitors. Take a look back to what you just wrote in section (a) of this exercise. Is that enough?

Remember, the only way to make headway with a 'me-too' product, is to make it outstandingly better and different.

Now write down any new ideas below:—

EXERCISE 8

My planned marketing mix

So far in this chapter, you have considered various possible changes to your marketing-mix. It is very important not to just leave these random thoughts lying around. Far better to do something about it! You are a businessman—you make business decisions. So why not make your marketing-decisions right now! You should have most of the necessary information from the exercises.

Please write down what marketing-mix you plan to introduce for your product *within the next 6 months.*

Again, well done! You have now completed the second stage of ISP. You have taken the decision to *S*atisfy your consumers' needs.

As mentioned earlier in this book, this second stage in marketing (the action bit) is largely automatic. You probably found that in this chapter. It really depends on how well you completed the first *I*nformation stage.

The last part of ISP is *P*rofit. This comes mainly as a result of doing the first two parts well. But just to help you on your way, and to make sure you do achieve higher profitability, the rest of this book deals in turn with particular elements of marketing which businessmen find most difficult to carry out efficiently. Each of the following chapters will contain specific guidelines and tips related to a particular part of the marketing function.

In the meantime, the marketing-mix you have just planned, should be 'put on ice'. We will return to it at the end of the book —to make final adjustments and modifications.

CHAPTER SIX

HOW MUCH CAN I SELL?

How well are we going to do next week, next month, next year? How many units can we sell? Can you put a number on the future? Your whole financial plan depends on the number you come up with. Your standing with the bank manager depends on it—and ultimately your own peace-of-mind!

Perhaps (I can hear you thinking) McMahon will come up with the magic formula to produce this magic number. He won't! There is no magic formula. What I will come up with however, is the simplest (and most reliable) approach to producing the magic number.

Sure, there are lots of complicated statistical techniques you can use for sales forecasting. The textbooks are full of them. They are all based on the idea of extrapolation. In other words you take your sales figures for, say, the last five years. You look at the trend from five years ago to the present. Then you use one of many statistical formulae to extrapolate (or continue) this trend into the future.

What the formula tells you then is that *if* the historical market trend does continue into the future, and *if* both you and your competitors continue to do much the same sort of thing as you did in the past, and *if* everything else remains equal . . . . . it is *likely* that you will sell *x* thousand units. There are a lot of 'ifs', aren't there? Still, you would have some sort of figure. It would probably be better than having no figure—at least as a first step.

So which of the many statistical formulae is the best? One of my colleagues at the Irish Management Institute, Tony Moynihan, based his doctoral thesis on this very problem. What he did was take a group of experienced marketing managers and give each of them a set of fictitious historical sales figures. He then asked each of them to produce a sales forecast. They were free to play around with the figures any way they liked—and then come up with their own 'hunch' or estimate of future sales. None of them used a statistical technique! Tony then extrapolated the same historical sales data using all known statistical techniques. He then compared the 'guesstimates' of experienced marketing managers with the forecasts based on statistical methods. He wanted to see how big a difference there would be between the 'guesstimates' and the mathematical forecasts. Maybe you've guessed the result! He found *no significant difference.*

So the message is that the estimate of an experienced manager is as reliable as statistical sales forecasting.

Who, then, uses all these statistical sales forecasting techniques you may ask. In my experience, those few managers who use these techniques, do so mainly to dazzle their bosses and colleagues with their technical brilliance! Or else they use the techniques selectively to justify a figure which they have already arrived at by hunch. I am speaking here, of course, about some marketing executives in large corporations. But don't get me wrong! Many of the larger multinational marketing corporations use experience-based estimates. They tried the complicated mathematical approach at one time or another, and now find that experienced-based estimates are just as reliable—and take less time!

So how should we tackle the problem of producing a sales forecast? Here's the method. It comprises six steps.

Step 1. Total market figures

Try to get the total market figure for the product category (in units and/or money value) for the last five years (including this year). It sounds like a tall order! It is. But here are a few ways of going about it. Try the statistics office, or government department which deals with trade. They may have the figures ready-made for you. Alternatively you could try the chamber of commerce or your own trade association.

Another idea worth thinking about is coming to an information-sharing arrangement with your competitors. The idea here is that each competitor sends in his own (three-monthly) sales figures to a mutually acceptable independent body. Perhaps your own trade association could organise it. Or you could use a firm of auditors. The auditors would then post out to each contributing firm only the total sales figure for each three-month period. Thus *you* would know your own market-share and the size of the total market. You would then have to guess the shares of competitive brands.

If none of the above methods work for you—then, as a last resort, you would have to pay for this information. There is no harm in approaching a small market research agency to find out how much it would cost you. At this stage then, you make a judgment. Would it be worth the money? Only you can answer this one.

Step 2. Plot the trend into the future

You simply write down the total market figures for the past five years. Draw a sales graph. Look at the line and judge how the line is likely to continue into the future. This will give you a first shot at what next year's total market should be.

If you want to be more scientific about it (and if you are any way mathematically inclined) there are two aids you could use from the world of mathematics. They are semi-logarithmic graph-paper or moving annual totals. Any beginner's book on statistics will explain these for you.

Step 3. Adjust your future trend figure, if necessary

Let us say you have carried out Step 2. You now have a figure for next year's total market sales. But this figure will only come true *if* the trend of the last five years continues. It will only occur *if* all the forces operating in your market continue as they have in the past. But, as you and I well know, next year *won't* be quite the same as this year!

So what you have to do now is use your *judgment*—as a businessman, as an observer of human nature, as a man who 'knows' his market. What you are really asking yourself is: 'Will the figure I projected in Step 2 actually occur? Or will some influences in the market-place knock the graph a bit up or down? Which influences—competitors' activity, my activity, a change in government regulations, a change in the number of customers in the market, new import/export legislation, a new fashion trend, a new industry trend, a change in technology, a change in distribution patterns, etc.? If next year's figure will be different from that projected—by what per cent will it be different?'

You then write down your adjusted figure (if adjusted) for next year's total market. Hopefully you will have it in terms of both units sold and money value.

Step 4. Your own product sales figures

Simply dig into your own records, and collect the sales figures (units and money) for your own product over the last five years.

Step 5. Plot your sales into the future

As you already have total market sales for each year, you can now express your sales as a percentage of the total market. So you can now plot a new graph for the last five years–in terms of your *market share.* Do two graphs, while you're at it–one showing the trend in your share of the market in terms of volume, and the other showing your market share in terms of money spent.

Extend these two graphs into the future–just as you did in Step 2.

What if you weren't able to get total market figures in the first place? In that case you just have to project your own sales trend into the future. The figure you get will probably be less useful (because it won't be based on your market share). But the figure you get in this case will at least be better than just making a wild guess.

Step 6. Adjust your projected sales figure as necessary.

The figures you have from Step 5 show you what your market share will be *if* everything continues much the same as in the past.

So just as in Step 3, you use your judgment again. What effort will these market influences have on your projected share?

And now we come to the crunch. Up to now we have been seeing our future sales as being determined by the 'Market Gods'. But we now come to the part where *you* decide to influence the market, instead of the other way around.

In Exercise 8 in the previous chapter, you wrote down your *planned marketing-mix* for one product for next year. Hopefully that mix is an improvement on this year's one. So . . by what per cent will you lift that projected sales figure as a result of your new mix?

You write down your adjusted market shares for next year. These figures are a result of forecasting and planned action.

Translate these share figures into absolute volume and money terms.

Having read through those six steps above, it would be a good idea to put them into practice as soon as you can. Why not continue working on the product you picked originally? Why not prepare a sales plan for next year now?

CHAPTER SEVEN

PRODUCTS, PRICES AND PROFITS

Every year, when you get your accounts done, you find out how much profit you made. In all probability you sell more than one product. So which of your products brings in most of those profits? Which of your products are more profitable than others? Indeed, which of your products are actually making a loss?

It would be useful to get answers to these questions, for two reasons. Firstly, you would be better able to decide for which of your products you should spend more money on marketing—and also which products you should merely carry, or indeed drop altogether. Secondly, such information about product profitability is essential for planning your marketing-mix. (Remember ISP!) You need it particularly as an aid to deciding the *price* of each of your products.

As a rule, most businessmen like to price a particular product so that the price itself covers all costs incurred in producing the product (or service) *plus* a certain margin for profits. So first of all you need to find out how much your product actually costs!

COSTING YOUR PRODUCT

There are two types of costs incurred in producing a product: direct costs and indirect costs. Let's just clarify what is meant by these terms.

Direct costs are all the costs you could 'put a finger on' and allocate to a particular product. A good way to get a fix on these costs is to ask yourself: 'If I were to produce and sell just one more (of the particular product), what *extra* costs would I incur?' Direct costs are often subdivided into two categories—labour costs and materials costs.

Sometimes direct costs are referred to as variable costs—because they vary! In other words, the more you produce, the more of these costs you incur. If you increase production by five per cent, your total bill for labour and materials will go up. However, not all costs will increase. And these are the other ones we need to look at.

Indirect costs are the costs which you can't easily allocate to any one particular product. Cost items such as office salaries, general maintenance, heating and *your own salary* would fall into this broad category. Very often these costs are referred to as *fixed* costs (as opposed to variable). In other words, you have to pay more or less the same fixed sum whether you increase production by five per cent or not.

It is virtually impossible to find a perfect way of allocating these costs to the different products produced. For example, say you produce only three different products. What proportion of *your salary* (indirect or fixed cost) should each of these three products bear? Difficult, isn't it?

Another popular term for indirect costs is overhead costs. From now on I will refer only to direct costs and overhead costs.

So what should you do about all this? In my opinion, you should hire a costing clerk or accountant as soon as you can afford one. If you can't afford one, full-time, you need to get one of your clerks to keep cost records—or even do it yourself.

There is little problem about allocating direct costs. But, as mentioned already, allocating overhead costs usually is a problem. It can be even more of a problem when it comes to pricing decisions.

Let's take an over-simplified example—just to make the point. Let us imagine that the data in Figure 7 below, refer to your company.

Let us further imagine that you sell three products. You can allocate direct costs to them easily enough. But how should you allocate overheads? What the accountant would do in this case is invent a 'formula' for allocating overheads.

He would look at the figures in Figure 7 and look for some sort of relationship between overhead costs and other costs. The formula would be based on the total company figures. He would then apply this formula to each of your three product-lines. In this example, he might come up with three (or more) formulae—see Figure 8.

Figure 7

Projected (total company) financial data for the coming year, are as follows:—

Direct Costs	Labour	$100,000
	Materials	$200,000
	Overhead Costs	$150,000
	Total Costs	$450,000
	Profit Target (10% mark-up on total costs)	$ 45,000
	Total Sales Revenue Target	$495,000

Figure 8

Formula A. $$\text{Overhead Costs} = \frac{(\text{Labour} \times 3)}{2}$$

Formula B. $$\text{Overhead Costs} = \frac{(\text{Materials} \times 3)}{4}$$

Formula C. $$\text{Overhead Costs} = \frac{(\text{Labour} + \text{Materials})}{2}$$

Now let's see what happens, when it comes to costing your three products. See Figure 9 below.

Figure 9

Costs per Unit

	Product 1	*Product 2*	*Product 3*
	$	$	$
(Direct) Labour	4.00	10.00	30.00
(Direct) Materials	16.00	8.00	5.00
Direct cost	20.00	18.00	35.00
Formula A			
Overhead cost	6.00	15.00	45.00
Total cost	$ 26.00	$ 33.00	$ 80.00
Formula B			
Overhead cost	12.00	6.00	3.75
Total cost	$ 32.00	$ 24.00	$ 38.75
Formula C			
Overhead cost	10.00	9.00	17.50
Total cost	$ 30.00	$ 27.00	$ 52.50

See what happens? Depending on the formula you use, you get a different total cost figure each time! And if, say, your pricing policy is '10 per cent mark-up on total cost', you could (in the case of Product 3) end up with a selling-price of $88.00 or $42.63 or $57.75. So which price should you charge??? Who knows? There are really two main messages from all of this:

1. Allocate as many *direct* costs to each product as possible. Then take a close look at each cost item in your total company overheads. It may be possible to reasonably allocate certain items by product. Only you can decide if these allocations make sense. For example, you may be able to allocate fairly, certain of your *factory overheads,* such as machine costs (if each machine is used for a particular product) or advertising costs (if each product is advertised separately).
2. After you have allocated as many costs as you can to each product—stop! Then consider the following relationship:

   (Sales revenue for Product 1)—(Product 1 direct costs)+(as many overhead costs as you can fairly allocate to Product 1) = Product 1 contribution to overhead.

In other words, there will still be a lot of overhead costs which you cannot really allocate fairly among your various products. So what should you do about these overhead costs which are left over?

When you are dealing with each of your products individually, *forget* about those overheads. Instead, think in terms of the nearest you can get to product profitability. And the nearest you can get is the concept of *contribution to overhead costs* (as per the above formula).

Now, of course, your *contribution* for each product will not only pay for some of your total overheads but *also* hopefully (but not always) bring in a genuine *profit* in the accounting sense.

When it comes to reviewing and planning the performance of any one of your products, *contribution to overhead* is the only measure which really makes sense. In marketing terms, the 'P' in ISP really stands for contribution to overhead. However, when it comes to reviewing and planning for your *total company,* you have to make sure that, when you add up the contributions of all your products, you not only cover all your overhead costs, but also that there is enough left over to give you a handsome profit!

NOW ABOUT PRICING YOUR PRODUCT

A pricing decision is like a balancing act. There are two sides to the pricing coin. One side you consider is the cost of your product and the contribution you want. The other side is the market—how much will your customers buy at various price levels? You want to strike a balance with a price which will give you *not* the highest unit sales figures, and *not* the highest sales revenue figures, but the *highest contribution to overhead!*

As with most marketing decisions, it's very difficult to be systematic and exact. There are so many variables and complex interrelationships involved. Nevertheless, what I will now do is put ten questions to you. Each of these questions is designed to stimulate the sort of thinking which is necessary, in order to arrive at a pricing decision. Think again of the marketing-mix you outlined already at the end of chapter 5. You now want to finally decide on the price for this product . . .

1. What sort of price would blend best with the rest of my marketing-mix?

In theory, there are two extreme types of marketing-mix. One extreme is the luxury mix—top quality/luxury/prestige image plus heavy advertising to promote this image plus high price (to pay for the advertising and justify the image). The other extreme is the bread and butter image—average or below average quality plus 'me-too' image plus low price (i.e. customers only buy it because it's the cheapest).

Where does *your* mix fit in, between these two extremes? Where is it on the spectrum? Remember, it is relatively easy to sell a high quality product at a low price. But it is very, very difficult to sell a low quality product at a high price! 'Tell me something I don't know already!', I can hear you saying. But think about it. How often do businessmen make this very mistake! The marketing graveyard is full of low-quality products which tried to get away with a high price. This point is yet another of the great marketing 'truths'. And, as you have probably realised by now, all the great marketing 'truths' are no more than simple common-sense.

Very often your customers will have a certain price-range in mind when they buy your type of product. For instance, imagine you were selling men's ties. Your customers might normally think in terms of paying from $4 to $8 for a tie. This ($4 – $8) range is known as the 'reference price-range'. Now the point is that if your price actually falls outside this range (even by a small amount) your product may be regarded as *very* cheap or *very* expensive. So if it's priced at $3.99, it's a very cheap tie. If it's $8.28, it's very expensive.

Very often (particularly with inflation) the reference price range is lower than the actual current price range in the market— or vice versa. This can create marketing opportunities for you.

2. How much will my product cost to produce?

We have already dealt with costing methods in some detail in this chapter. What you need to do is establish the direct costs involved plus as many 'allocatable' overhead costs as you can for the product in question. This will give you a total cost picture.

Let's go back to those men's ties again. Let us further imagine that your costing information is as follows:

Labour (divide the wages you pay in a particular time period by the average number of ties produced in that period): = $2.00 per tie.

Materials (divide the cost of tie-making materials you buy in by the average number of ties produced from it): = $0.50 per tie.
Total direct costs: = $2.50 per tie.

'Allocatable' overhead costs (annual rental of special tie-making machine): = $2,000.

Now what you can do is plot a simple cost chart to show you what all of this means, at a glance. To do this for your own real products, buy a pad of simple graph-paper at any stationery shop.

If you look now at Figure 10 below, you will see the cost chart for the above data.

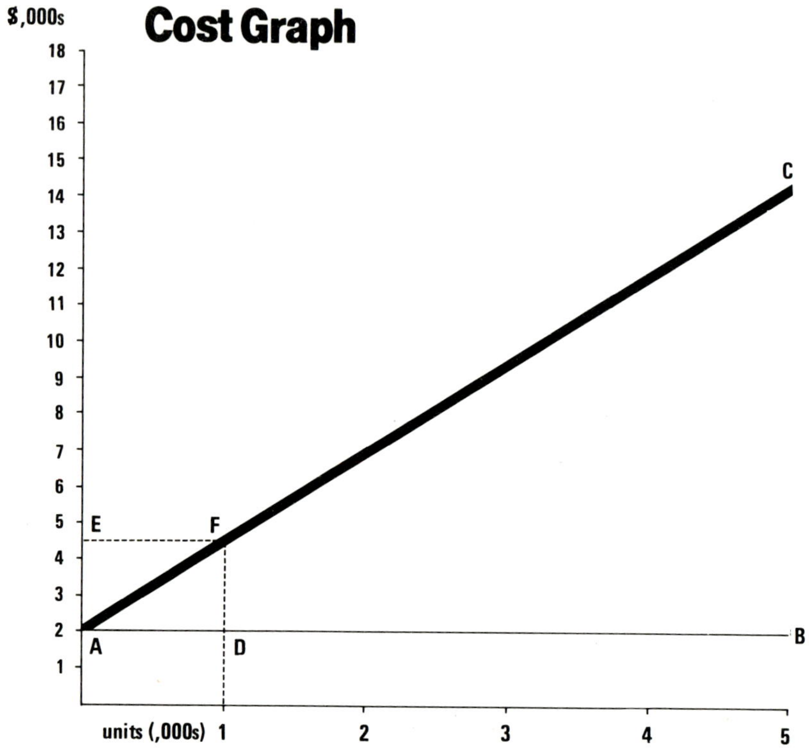

Figure 10

The horizontal axis on the graph represents the number of units you could produce (in thousands of units). The vertical axis represents the money it would cost (in thousands of dollars).

The first line you plot on the graph is for your *'allocatable' overhead costs.* You know that whether you produce no ties, or two ties or 3,000 ties you will be stuck with the same fixed cost of $2,000 per year. So this line will be a straight horizontal line, as AB in Figure 10.

Next, you need to plot the line for your *direct costs.* These are the costs which are variable. The more you produce, the more it will cost you. Now in this case your direct costs will be $2.50 for every unit produced. And you will incur these costs on top of the 'allocatable' overhead which you are stuck with anyway. So imagine you were to produce 1,000 ties. That would give you a direct cost of $2,500. Move along the AB line to 1,000 units (D on the graph). Draw a dotted vertical line up from D.

Then move up the money axis from point A ($2,000) until you get an extra $2,500 at point E. Draw a dotted horizontal line across from point E. The two dotted lines intersect at point F.

Then join A to F and continue the straight line out. This line AC now represents your total costs for these ties. Have a go at doing this cost-chart for yourself on a spare piece of paper.

Let us leave costing for now. We'll be coming back to it again at the end of this chapter.

3. Do your customers see your product as 'different' from your competitors', or 'much the same'?

This is an important question in terms of pricing. If your product is seen as *'much the same'* (i.e. a 'me-too' product), then you have very little pricing freedom. If you raise your price, nobody will buy your product. Why should they? After all, they can get just as good a product from your competitors for less money.

If you lower your price, you will gain a big advantage, at first. But your competitors are probably in much the same situation as yourself. So they will be forced to lower their prices also. And if that happens, you're worse off than before. You're selling just as much—but your profit margins are lower. In other words, you can easily slip into a price-war.

But maybe customers do see your product as *'different'* in some way. Your product may have a 'perceived difference'. The real, physical difference between your product and your competitors' is *not* what's important. The important difference is that which is *perceived* by your customers. Thus Lux toilet soap may be physically much the same as any other, but it is perceived as being different by consumers.

What you must do is decide what exactly the perceived difference is for your product. Then ask yourself whether customers would be prepared to pay a bit extra for this perceived difference. In other words, can you slap a price-tag on it?

And, of course, if yours is a 'me-too' product, can you do anything to create a perceived difference? Perhaps you can do this by changing some other element in your marketing-mix, such as product design, packaging or advertising.

4. To what extent (if any) is your price a quality or status indicator?

If I went out to buy a refrigerator tomorrow, I would not be able to judge which machine to buy, on a technical basis. However, if I see one refrigerator priced at $200 and another at $400, I would probably conclude that the $400 one was the better quality machine. After all, if it costs more I suppose it must be better . . . ?

In many markets, there is a psychological link (in customers' minds) between price and quality. And when the customer cannot technically evaluate a product, he will fall back on other quality indicators, such as *price.*

Similarly, with status. If I am looking for status when I buy a car or a suit of clothes, the higher the price the greater the status! With most products, if you raise the price, you expect to sell less. But, as you well know, if you raise the price on a prestige product you might actually sell more!

5. If you change your price, how will your competitors react?

Your competitors are no fools. It's always safer to imagine them as being at least as clever, if not more so, than yourself!

6. Are you trying to break into a new market?

If so, think about the critical role your price might play. You might decide that the only way to break in would be on a low price basis. Alternatively, you might enter with a high price, in order to 'skim the cream' off the top end of the market.

Remember though, that it's easier later on to move down from a high price than vice-versa!

7. Are you selling a product range?

If so, it can sometimes make sense to price one item in the range very low (even below cost). This low-priced item can then be used to get new accounts. You would hope later to make money from these accounts by selling them your more profitable items. This type of pricing is very popular in the retail trade (e.g. the 'loss-leader' type of promotion in supermarkets).

8. Are you happy with your current approach to pricing?

Let's look at the three most popular pricing habits in industry today.

(a) *Cost-Plus Pricing:* The formula for this is:

Product costs + % mark-up = Product price.

Very often firms include some percentage of their total overheads in the product costs figure. I hope you are convinced by now that this practice is wrong. So let's amend the formula a bit:

Direct costs + allocatable overheads only + % mark-up = Price.

The formula is still inadequate because it is too product-oriented! Who says you can get this same fixed percentage mark-up on every product you make? The problem here is that we are only looking at one side of the coin. We should also be looking at the other side—the market. What price will the market bear? We'll be back to this question shortly.

In the meantime let's change that formula around a bit:

> Contribution to overhead = price — (direct costs + Allocatable overheads).

It looks better now, doesn't it?

(b) *Mark-Up Pricing:* This pricing practice applies in the retail trade. It's a variation on Cost-Plus pricing. It goes like this:

> Cost of bought-in item + standard % mark-up = price.

Each branch of retailing tends to have its own sacrosanct standard mark-up. Obviously the jeweller's is higher than the grocer's. The mark-up is intended to cover all other costs such as storage, wages, interest, etc. and leave a margin for profit.

Again this approach is too product-oriented. The successful retailer today is often the man who breaks the rules. He does not accept that the standard trade mark-up should apply to him!

(c) *'Me-Too' Pricing:* This is another popular one. 'If my competitors are charging $9 to $11 for their products, then I'd better stay within that range for mine. My competitors have found that this is the most profitable price to charge. I guess they should know. If I charge a higher price, nobody will buy. If I charge a lower price maybe I won't cover my costs. Or worse, I might start a price-war. It's better to play it safe—and not rock the boat!'

This approach has at least the virtue of being oriented towards your competitors (not your customers, of course!). But who says you shouldn't rock the boat occasionally? Must you always follow the herd?

Remember, you're stuck with the cost of renting that machine anyway. You're also stuck with all your other overhead costs. And every little bit helps!

The fact that you increase production may even help reduce your direct costs per unit.

The cost of producing one extra tie should be at least covered by the price you charge. And in this case, the marginal extra cost is of course $2.50.

How do you get away with this, without offending your existing customers? After all, if they have to pay $5.00 per tie, and you now come out with one priced at $2.60! What you do is sell to a different market or make the product appear different.

9. Have you got spare production capacity?

I guess you probably have. The fact that you bought this book—and have stuck with it this far!—indicates that you need marketing. And it's a fact of life that the businessmen who need marketing most are those with spare capacity!

Let's go back to those men's ties again (we looked at them in Question 2 above). Let's say your total annual production capacity is 4,000 ties. But, say, you can only sell 3,000 at a particular price (say *$5.00*).

Remember the direct cost per unit? It was $2.50 per tie. Now of course you'd like to sell more ties on top of the 3,000 you sell already. What price should you charge for these extra ties. As much as you can get naturally. But the point is that selling them at any price is worthwhile—as long as the price you get is *more than $2.50.*

This is known as the marginal approach. When you are using up spare capacity, any price is worthwhile as long as you at least cover your direct costs, and *make some contribution to overhead*—no matter how small!

10. Which price will be the most profitable for you?

This is the crunch question. This is where you have to balance your costs with market demands—and come up with the price which gives you the best contribution to overhead.

Again—back to the ties. We already have the cost structure in Figure 10.

What you do next is produce a number of sales forecasts, at different prices. We looked at forecasting in chapter 6, remember. But this time you do more than one—showing how much you think you will sell, at different prices.

You then relate these sales forecasts to the cost structure you have already. To see the implications at a glance, you can draw up a *Break-Even Chart.* In fact we have one half-completed already in Figure 10. We have drawn the cost-line AC. All we need to do now is draw the line representing *revenue.*

So let's imagine we make the following forecasts:

Price	*Sales Forecasts (Units)*	*Revenue Forecasts (Units) x (Price)*
$4.50	3,500	$15,750
$5.00	3,000	$15,000
$5.50	2,000	$11,000

At first glance, it looks as if $4.50 is the best price to charge. At $4.50 we sell more ties and bring in more revenue. But do remember, its the *most profitable* price we're after. Specifically we want the price which gives us the highest contribution to overhead. The price which brings in the highest sales figures is not necessarily the price which is most profitable.

So let's look at our *Break-Even Chart* now (see Figure 11 opposite).

We have taken the second possible price of $5.00 and drawn a revenue line. How we do it is to move along the horizontal (units) axis until we reach 3,000 (point K). Then we move up the vertical ($) axis until we reach $15,000 (point L). We join K and L at point M. Then draw a straight line GM.

GM is your Revenue line. X is your break-even point. From then on you're making money. PM is your contribution to overhead—in this case $5,500.

Have a go now at plotting in this revenue line yourself on the rough chart you have done already.

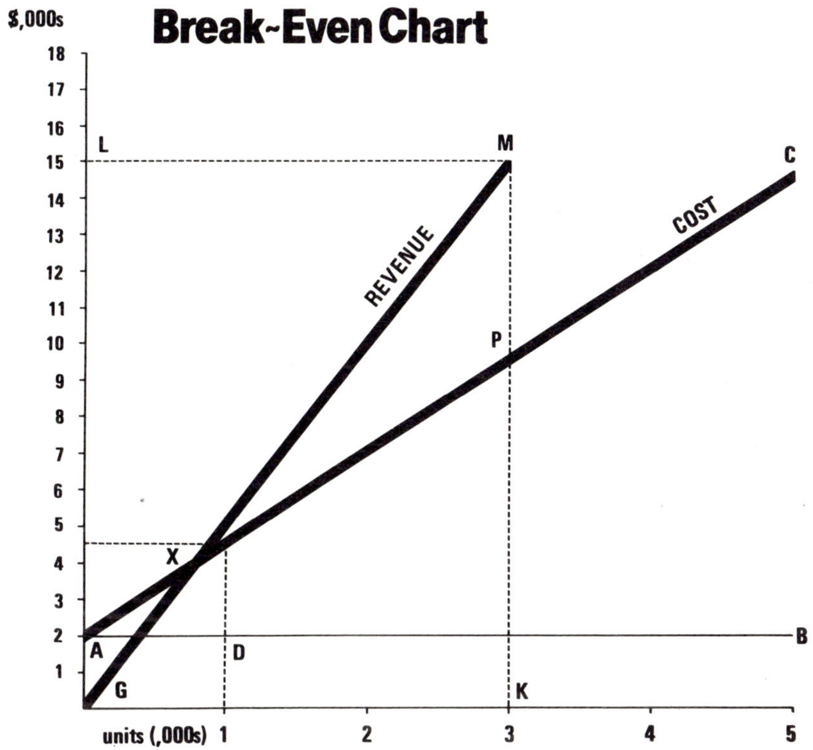

Figure 11

From then on, you do the same again for the other two prices—$4.50 and $5.50.

When we compare the results we find the following:

Price	Sales forecast (Units)	Revenue forecast (Units x Price)	Allocatable overhead costs	Direct costs (Units x $2.50)	Total costs	Contribution to overhead
$4.50	3,500	$15,750	$2,000	$8,750	$10,750	$5,000
$5.00	3,000	$15,000	$2,000	$7,500	$ 9,500	$5,500
$5.50	2,000	$11,000	$2,000	$5,000	$ 7,000	$4,000

Thus, the best price to set would be $5.00.

At the end of the previous chapter, I left you with the suggestion that you draw up your own sales forecasts, along the lines suggested. When you have done that, you should also continue working along the lines suggested in this chapter. In other words:

(a) You should find out the direct costs for your product.
(b) Isolate also any 'allocatable' overhead costs.
(c) Draw a cost chart.
(d) Reconsider the ten pricing questions in this chapter.
(e) Take a closer look at the price you already decided on in chapter 5. Do you want to change it or not?
(f) Do three sales forecasts, with a different price for each.
(g) Do three Break-Even Charts.
(h) Decide on the price which will give you the maximum contribution to overhead.

This has been a rather long chapter. It has also been rather technical. If the contents are not clear, it would be a good idea to go back through it again.

I can at least offer you one consolation. From now on this book will get progressively easier to digest!

CHAPTER EIGHT

NOW ABOUT PERSUASION . . . . .

Back at the end of chapter 5, you completed Exercise 8. This was your planned marketing-mix for the product you're working on with this book. As part of this exercise you described the *communications – mix* you intend to implement. This chapter, and the next three, will help you to improve this vital part of your mix.

But before going any further, please check back to what you wrote on page 74. Just read through it quickly, to refresh your memory.

Now let's think in terms of an overall communications strategy. After all, we have many 'weapons' at our disposal. We have selling, advertising, public relations, etc. How should we use these weapons? On which of them (if any) should we spend most effort and money? Above all, how should we make sure that all our persuasive weapons are acting in harmony to produce the desired result? And, of course, the desired end-result is increased sales and profitability. So how should we set about *persuading* our target customers to buy?

It is worth stating here that you can never *force* your customers to buy. All you can do is send 'messages' to them. If they actually receive these messages, then they may decide to buy! So really what we're about here is asking ourselves: 'In what form should these messages be transmitted?'.

Some years ago Russell Colley* wrote a very interesting book for the United States Association of National Advertisers. Although the book was written specifically for the major advertisers, it also contains material which is very helpful for putting together an overall strategy of persuasion. One model which Russell Colley puts forward is the 'Communications Spectrum'.

******Defining Advertising Goals for Measured Advertising Results,* **Russell H. Colley, US Association of National Advertisers.**

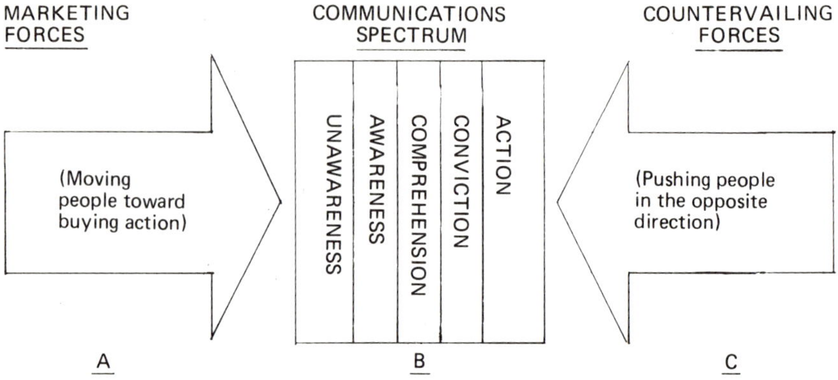

Figure 12

Section B of the above diagram represents the mental state of your customers—in relation to your particular product.

So let's imagine one of your potential customers . . .

—Is he *unaware* of your product's existence?
—Or does he know about it already—is he aware?
—Does he also understand or *comprehend* the product's features?
—Does he believe that yours is the right product for him—is he *convinced?*
—And finally, is he actually taking *action*—is he buying your product?

You could say that the minds of your customers are *floating* along this spectrum—from unawareness through to action. And they are also, to some extent, floating back in the opposite direction.

Over on the left-hand side (section A in the above diagram) you have your own marketing forces. These forces include selling, advertising, point-of-sale material, etc. These forces are pushing your customers' minds from unawareness towards action.

But, unfortunately, you also have section C, the countervailing forces. These include your competitors' activities, memory lapse, death, etc. These countervailing forces are pushing your customers back from action towards unawareness.

So, in a way, you have a ding-dong battle going on between

these forces. And in the middle you have the fickle minds of your customers, floating between the two extremes.

Why is this model helpful?

The 'Communications Spectrum' model is helpful because it assists you in assigning specific tasks to each element in your communications-mix. For example, you might decide that the task of your advertising is to move people from *unawareness* to *comprehension.* And that's all. (In other words,you don't try to do everything with your advertising.) And then the job of your salesmen is to reinforce comprehension and move them from *comprehension* to *action.*

Of course, in some cases you might well decide that the most efficient method would be to let one element do all the work. For example, you might opt for direct-mail advertising for an unknown product. And this is perhaps the most difficult form of advertising to undertake. Think of it. With one leaflet you have to start by telling them about the product, then take them all the way through the spectrum and then ask them for the order! It's difficult, but it can be done.

What this model does first of all is help clarify your strategic thinking.

How can I use it?

Let's go back to your own product again. Please do the following two short exercises.

EXERCISE 9

Think of your target customers. Then fill in the questions below. You'll have to guess the answers. But your guess will be based on experience, and it will probably be near enough to the exact truth.

Unawareness	What percentage of your target customers never heard of your product?	%
Awareness	What percentage are aware of it?	%
Comprehension	What percentage of them have a good understanding of your product's features?	%
Conviction	What percentage are convinced that your product meets their needs?	%
Action	What percentage of your target customers actually buy your product on a fairly regular basis?	%

Incidentally, if the categories in the spectrum don't suit your particular marketing situation, why not write in new categories to suit your business?

EXERCISE 10

Now think of the various possible 'weapons' you could use in your communications-mix. You won't use all of them. You may even decide to use only one. But more than likely, you'll decide on some sort of combination.

The idea in this exercise is that you describe the task of each element of your mix in terms of *moving your customers from one stage to another along the spectrum.*

Persuasive Weapons	The Task of this weapon is to move my customers . . . . .
Selling	From. . . . . to . . . .
Advertising	From. . . . . to . . . .
Public Relations	From. . . . . to . . . .
Sales Aids	From. . . . . to . . . .
Merchandising	From. . . . . to . . . .
Special Promotions	From. . . . . to . . . .

Cross out any weapons which you decide not to use.

You now have a general strategic framework for your communications-mix. Again, I know it's simple. But it's very necessary. You'll see the sense of it more clearly when we get to chapter 11.

CHAPTER NINE

HOW TO SELL

Virtually every man, who runs his own business, has to sell. In fact, when you think about it, you are your company's principal salesman. If your business has got to a certain size you may already have hired a number of full-time salesmen. But even still, you probably find that you still spend a lot of time selling for your company. All in all, selling is one of the most important elements in the marketing-mix for your products.

There are lots of experts on salesmanship around. Most of them are ex-salesmen who have developed their own personal style of selling. The trouble is, however, that many of these 'experts' disagree with each other. The truth is that when it comes to selling to *your* customers, the only real expert is *you.*

What I'll do in this chapter is confine myself to three areas. First, I'll describe what happens during a sales interview. Second, I'll tell you what researchers have found out about what it takes to sell successfully. And finally I'll finish the chapter with a list of 'do's and dont's'.

What happens when you sell?

Every sales interview is (or should be) a two-way conversation. Think of the times when other salesmen try to sell to you. I'm sure you'll agree that very often what happens is a boring monologue by the salesman. And, of course, you don't give him the order, do you? How rarely you find yourself as a *customer* taking an active, involved part in a sales interview!

And is it any different when you take your turn as salesman? Aren't many of your sales calls unsuccessful? Don't you find yourself (at least sometimes) delivering a boring, repetitive monologue to a weary hostile customer?

Take a look at this diagram.

When you start a sales call you usually have a pretty good idea what you intend to say. The sales presentation you have in mind will include product features and benefits as well as how you intend to make the various points. Each customer is different. So your knowledge of his business and personality will influence your planned presentation.

So let's say you start making your presentation. Then, sooner or later, the customer responds. He starts giving you *feedback.* This feedback could take many forms. It could be verbal or non-verbal. It could be a grunt, a yawn, a string of sentences. It could be silence, a particular tone of voice, the way he sits.

What this feedback does is update your knowledge of the customer. It tells you more about how the customer is feeling and thinking right now! Each customer is not only different—he changes from minute to minute. The more you know about him, the easier it is to talk to him in his own terms.

In the ideal situation, when you receive this feedback, you use it automatically to *adjust your presentation to suit this particular customer at this particular moment in time.* Thus each sales presentation you make should be different. Each presentation should be tailor-made for the customer in question.

This is why direct selling is a much more sophisticated form of persuasion than advertising. Advertising is not tailor-made for each customer. What you do when you advertise is send out the same message to everybody.

So to sell effectively, you must pick up this feedback and use it. This is what experienced salesmen do instinctively. To obtain better results there are two rules:

1. *Make sure you pick up the feedback.* In other words, don't talk too much—listen! If you talk all the time, how can you listen? Also observe with your eyes. Look at the customer. His facial expression and body posture will often tell you more than what he really says. Ask questions to give you more feedback.
2. *Use the feedback to adjust your presentation.* Don't just carry on with your planned speech, ignoring this new information. Remember it really is true that you are *not* selling to him. You should be *helping him to buy!* The presentation should be made from *his* point of view, addressing *his* needs as *he* sees them.

What can the researchers tell us?

The best type of research into selling has been based on 'live' data. In other words, the researcher sits in on real interviews and records hundreds of interviews and their results. He then analyses these data in order to draw general conclusions. Not all selling research is of this type, however.

Unfortunately, some research findings are pretty useless for the practising salesman. However, I have listed below nine broad findings which I believe are very useful for the practising salesman.

1. *The Ideal Salesman?* A lot of research money has gone into efforts to pin down the characteristics of this particular animal.

Most salesmen will be relieved to hear that the main result has been to show that there is no such creature as the ideal salesman! Or if he does exist, they haven't yet been able to put him into a psychological category!

However, there is some evidence which suggests that all successful salesmen do have one characteristic in common. That characteristic is *empathy.* In other words, the salesman who can genuinely see things 'through the customer's eyes' is usually more successful.

2. *Who should do the talking?* One interesting piece of research showed that the average salesman takes up more than 80 per cent of the conversation during a sales interview! The same piece of research showed that the more successful salesman takes up between 50 and 60 per cent of the conversation. It makes sense, doesn't it? If you talk all the time, you will find it almost impossible to pick up feedback. On the other hand, you do need to do a fair amount of talking. After all, you need to explain your product's benefits.

3. . . . . *And if you represent a small relatively unknown company?* You are at a disadvantage. If you have big, well-known competitors, they stand a better chance of getting in to see the buyer. They also have a better chance of getting a first order, or acceptance for a new product. Researchers refer to this as the *'Source Effect'.* Your own advertising and public relations activity can help to build up your company's source effect. The best way to do it is by consistently providing quality products and service over time. Word-of-mouth publicity is always the best.

On the other hand, although you may find it more difficult initially to get acceptance from a new customer, this disadvantage wears off over time. On your first call to a customer, he tends to 'see' your company first and you (if at all) second. But after building up the relationship over time, *you* become more important to the customer than your company.

So in this sense you are at least on a par with your bigger competitors . . . as far as your regular customers are concerned.

4. *What about product knowledge?* Research indicates that product knowledge is important. The salesman should know all

about the technicalities of the product he is selling. Many companies only train their salesmen in product knowledge. But be warned! Too much product knowledge can be a dangerous thing. Technical salesmen are often so much in love with their product that they are unable to see it from the customer's viewpoint. In other words, they can become too product-oriented!

And besides, we learn from research that the 'How' is usually more important than the 'What'. In other words, *how* the salesman presents his message is usually more important than *what* the message contains!

5. *How to spell out the benefits.* The man who has done most to clarify the nature of salesmanship is a British researcher, Neil Rackham. This point, as well as the next five, are his discoveries. According to Rackham, the salesman can make three types of references to his product:

(a) Features —when he mentions the technical or performance features of his product;
(b) Advantages —when he mentions how these features could possibly benefit the customer;

(c) Benefits —This is where the salesman mentions a particular advantage after the customer has already expressed a need (which this advantage satisfies).

Many sales-training courses teach people to keep mentioning product benefits. But what they are referring to really are advantages. Rackham's research points out the fallacy in this approach. The point is that Rackham's research shows clearly that the salesmen who most often mention benefits (as defined above) are the ones who have most successful calls.

6. *Asking questions.* Rackham further discovered that the salesmen who ask most questions also sell most. He also found that one particular type of question was more rewarding than others. And this was the type of question which explored the customer's decision guidelines. So, asking the customer how he feels about the coming football game is better than asking no questions at all. But it is far better to ask him how he feels about the type of delivery time he expects for your type of product!

Again, it makes sense. Questions bring feedback. And 'decision-guideline' questions bring even more useful feedback.

7. *How to handle customer objections.* This has been a major theme for years with writers and sales trainers. Rackham's research is now suggesting they may well have been wasting their energy. He has found that in successful sales interviews, customers raise few or no objections anyway!

8. *Closing the sale.* This has always been pictured as the dramatic moment at the end of the interview, when the salesman stops playing Mr. Nice Guy and actually gets up on his hind legs and asks for the order! Again, Rackham has found that many successful sales calls close themselves naturally. In other words, the customer gives the order as a natural conclusion to the interview. It's almost as if 'closing the sale' really depends on how you handle the other, earlier parts of the call.

9. *How to handle your most difficult customers.*

Take a look at this graph.

CUSTOMER TYPES

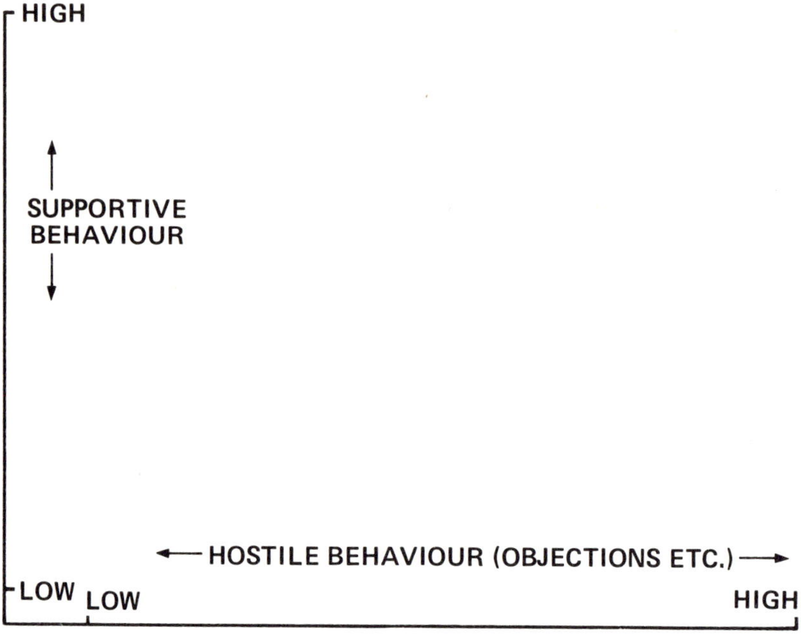

Figure 13

Consider your customers on two dimensions. The first (represented by the vertical axis) is *supportive behaviour.* Some of your customers are very low on this. Some are very high—they make nice friendly supportive noises in response to your sales approach. The other dimension is *hostile behaviour.* Again, some might be high or low on this.

Now, think of the type of customer who is (in your opinion) the most difficult to sell to? What combination has he of the behaviours on the graph? Is he high on supportive behaviour and low on hostile behaviour? Or is he medium on each? Put an "X" on the graph above to represent him. Then turn over to the next page for the answer!

CUSTOMER TYPES

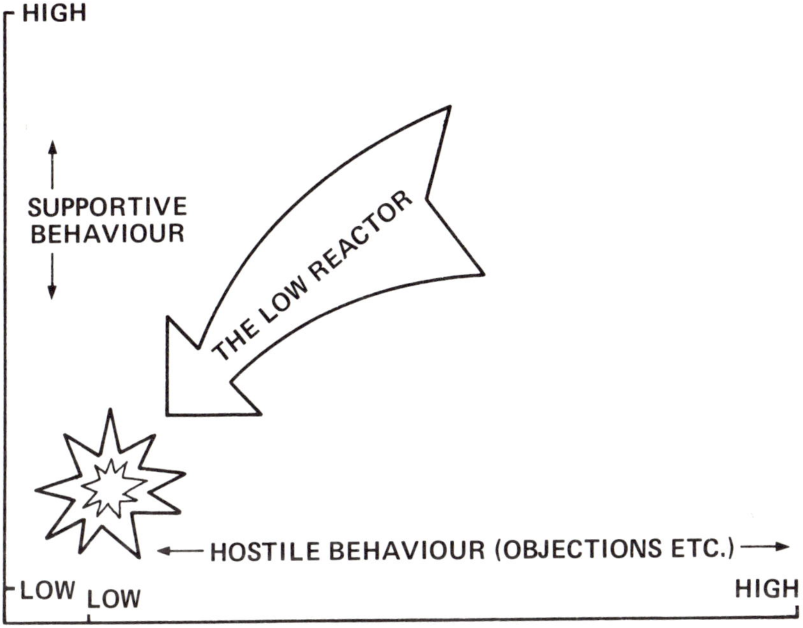

Figure 14

That's him above—the *Low Reactor.* He's low on both supportive *and* hostile behaviour. You've met him many times, haven't you?

The reason he's so difficult to sell to is that he starves you of feedback! You just don't know which way to play it with this character.

Rackham found that even the most experienced of salesmen 'fell to pieces' when they came up against this type of customer. Their rate of speech quickened. They repeated themselves more often. They even told more lies! They tended to make outlandish offers. Generally, they lost complete control of both themselves and the situation.

The funny thing is that when you meet a Low Reactor, you often incorrectly interpret his behaviour as hostile. You often find yourself getting extremely angry with him. And this doesn't do anyone any good.

The Low Reactor is often a professional buyer who has discovered that this is the most effective way to deal with salesmen! How right he is!

But how should *you* deal with *him?* There is only one way – *ask questions.* And keep asking questions! Eventually, he *must* respond. And then at least you will have some feedback on which to base your approach.

'Do's and don'ts' of selling.

1. *Know what you want to achieve, before the call.* Is this merely a preliminary 'softening-up' call? Do you want to leave your customer with a particular belief about your product? Are you looking for information? Do you want to get an order this time? If so, for how much?

2. *Plan your presentation beforehand.* Once you've decided on your specific objectives (as per above), this shouldn't be too difficult. But *don't* plan your presentation in a logical A – B – C – D sequence! If you do, it will only make your mind too stiff to react quickly to feedback. Because you will need to adjust your presentation, what you should do is plan the points you want to make and how you might make each point. Then you have a mental 'shelf' full of different points. As the interview progresses you take down and use whichever point seems most appropriate at the time.

3. *Remember, the first few minutes are usually the most important part of a sales interview!* A funny thing happens at the start of an interview (particularly with a new potential customer). It's like a battle between you and the customer. And only one of you can win! It goes like this.

Either:

(a) The salesman convinces the customer that he (the salesman) is worth listening to;

or

(b) The customer convinces the salesman that he (the salesman) is wasting his time.

Very often the course of the whole interview is pretty well decided after the first few minutes! So plan this first part of your presentation very carefully!

4. *Listen to your customer, and observe him as much as possible.* This is your first source of feedback.

5. *Adjust your presentation continually.* This is how you use your feedback. Either change course to follow the concerns of your customer. Or use the opportunity to make one of the points from your 'mental shelf'.

6. *Try to see things from your customer's viewpoint.* Think with him! (empathy).

7. *Don't talk too much!* Remember, no more than 60 per cent of the conversation should be taken up by you!

8. *Beware of 'Product–Fixation'.* Don't forget, your customer is more interested in the benefits your product can give him, than in its technicalities. The technicalities (i.e. features) should be used to support or prove the benefits.

9. *Ask questions (and keep asking them)!* This is one of the most important 'Do's'. It's your second source of feedback. From my own experience, the best questions to ask are those which explore the customer's opinions. Even 'Low Reactors' can't resist questions like these!

10. *Push those benefits!* In the fifth research finding (mentioned earlier in this chapter) I explained the difference between features, advantages and *benefits.* Benefits are what count. But, of course, in order to judge which are the real benefits, you need first to listen, observe and question!

A word about sales training.

In the 'Do's and Don'ts' above, you have ten guidelines to improve your selling success. But you'll notice that most of these are really *skills,* and to improve on any skill, the best way to learn is by practice. So if you are thinking of attending (or sending one of your salesmen to) a sales training course, do find out more about the the training methods used, beforehand. The course will be of little benefit unless it enables you to practise these skills in near-reality situations.

CHAPTER TEN

HOW TO MANAGE YOUR SALESMEN

This chapter is intended for you, if you have (or are planning to employ) your own sales force. If you don't fall into this category, you may prefer to skip to chapter 11.

What sort of people are they?

This is the best question to start with. After all, if we are to manage a particular group of people—the more we know about them, the better. So let's take a look at the nature of the selling job, and the people who do it.

Certainly it's a high-stress job. There are a few reasons for this. First of all, there's the *loneliness* element in the job. Most other people in organisations work in groups. The salesman works alone. And not only is he alone, but he does most of his work away from the office. The office-worker can at least feel some 'security' in the fact that he is working in his own 'territory'. The salesman works in 'enemy territory'. He often feels most alone when he comes away after a successful sales call—and there's nobody out there to applaud. Or worse still, when he staggers out after a disastrous call, there's nobody to pick up the pieces and help him to have enough courage and enthusiasm for his next encounter.

I mentioned empathy in the previous chapter. What this means in practice is that, when the salesman is calling on an aggressive business-like customer, then *he too* is 'aggressive and business-like'—*for the duration of that call!* But twenty minutes later he may be calling on an affable, sport-loving customer. So the salesman changes this role to 'affable and sport-loving'! The salesman must role-play. There is nothing necessarily phony about this. After all, everybody plays different roles. To your acquaintances, the 'you' they meet at work is different from the 'you' they meet at home. So you play at least two different roles. No problem.

But think of the salesman who must play ten to twenty different roles each day with different customers! This *changing of roles* is also stress-inducing.

Let me digress a little here into the realm of psychology, to explain my next point. Every individual has a concept of himself—his self-image. It is unclear—and based largely on childhood data. The child begins to form his self-concept by proving to his parents that he is the sort of person they think he is or expect him to be. The self-concept becomes more stable in adulthood. In many ways, it is a sense of competence/self-worth. Although my self-concept may be unclear, one thing I do know is that I am nearly always the 'goodie' related to my environment. And you're the same, dear reader! You feel you are basically an 'O.K. guy'. Everybody feels he's an 'O.K. guy'—except for some unfortunates in mental hospitals.

The point is that most people can be pushed around a bit—as long as you don't attack their self-concept! When their self-concept is attacked they become surly, hostile—even violent! The most precious possession each individual has is his 'self-concept'. He must always defend and preserve it.

Now think of the salesman. Let's say he makes fifteen calls a day. Chances are that during more than half of these calls, he gets messages from his customers such as:

'I'm too busy to see you!'
'Sorry, we don't buy rubbish!'
'Look you're wasting my time—and yours!'
'I might see you in an hour's time, if you wait around.'
'Why the hell are your deliveries always two days late?'
'Sorry, your prices are too high'.
'Look I'll give you five minutes to say your piece—and no more!'
etc., etc., etc. . . . .

All of these messages really add up to one total message—'I'm more important than you. And I like neither your products nor you. So clear off!'. That adds up to a lot of damage to one's self-concept in one day. And the salesman can't hit back. He has to take it.

This particular aspect of his job is probably the most stress-inducing. And not everybody can take it. Psychologists would call a selling job a 'high psychological-risk' job—because the self-concept gets so much punishment.

And it can be twice as bad for the poor salesman when he gets back to the office. Perhaps he staggers in, trying ro recover from his customers' abuse, only to get another litany of abuse from *you*—his boss!

Most salesmen nowadays get a company car. There is a very practical reason for this, of course. But there is another reason. That is to compensate the salesman for his lack of social status! Ask any salesman what he'd like his son to be when he grows up. Will he answer: 'a salesman, of course'? I doubt it. The salesman is only too well aware of the relatively low esteem in which he is held by customers, neighbours and even (sad to say) sometimes his family. Again more damage to his self-concept!

All in all, it sounds like a pretty unattractive way to earn a living, doesn't it? So why on earth do people become salesmen? The truth is that the salesman often falls into the job, by accident. Perhaps he failed to get into university. Or maybe he found himself working as a clerk—and the only way out of that rut was to get into selling. Very often he becomes a salesman because it's the only possible way for him to earn a reasonable salary.

So why does he stay in such a job? Let's face it, many salesmen stay selling for the whole of their working life. Some of them even get to enjoy it as a job. So where do they get their kicks? They enjoy the status elements such as car and expenses. Very often the money is good. They get a sense of achievement in making things happen. There's also the sense of responsibility—they do represent the company and (in a very real sense) they carry the company. When they win an order, there is a sense of power (albeit temporary) over the customer ('I *made* him buy!'). They also have to be creative and flexible in their thinking—there is less routine. Many of them simply enjoy being out and meeting people. And there is also the fact that, like most people, salesmen also actually like to work!

So, like most occupations, selling has its good and bad points. It's a balancing act. If the good points outweigh the bad ones, the salesman stays selling. The balancing act would look a bit like the diagram below.

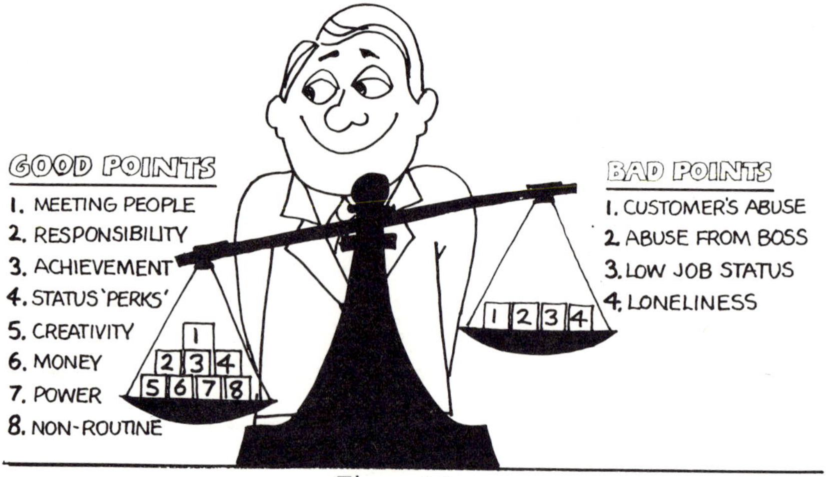

Figure 15

How should they be managed for best results?

There now follows a list of tips. These tips are based on a lot of research (including some of the author's) and the experience of sales managers, as monitored by the IMI.

Give them *as much responsibility as possible.* In other words, treat them as adults and not as children. To perform well, salesmen need to feel respected and trusted by their boss. For example, when it comes to planning, they should have an important say in setting their own sales targets. You may have already arrived at a total target sales figure for the company. It's not good enough just to divide it up among the salesmen and expect them to achieve it. They find that kind of treatment 'de-motivating'. They must also be given the opportunity to say what they will sell. Then, even if you have to agree on a compromise figure, at least each salesman feels he has some ownership of his sales target. Incidentally, the best form of target is stated in terms of the salesman's contribution to overhead. But more about that later.

Don't be a bully! You just can't get more output from salesmen these days by using coercion or authority. Dictators are out of date (in business anyway!). You (and they) should see you as being there to *help* them achieve their targets. You should persuade and help.

Expect high performance (and show it). This can have a powerful and positive effect on the salesmen's attitudes.

Show them that you too can sell. Salesmen like to see that the 'old man' can sell with the best of them, when necessary. But be careful about this one. Don't overdo it. Remember you hired *them* to do the selling so that you would have more time to manage the business. And they won't thank you for butting-in on their area of responsibility, or for showing-off!

Be their *'protector'.* One hears a lot of talk about company loyalty. Most people aren't loyal to an impersonal organism such as a company. But they can be loyal to a person (i.e. their immediate superior). But there's a *quid pro quo* involved here. They will feel loyal to you, if they feel that you are basically on their side. So you have to stand up for them—if necessary even against customers!

Salesmen don't want their boss to be a 'softie'. But they do expect him to be fair and honest in his dealings with them. So the message is: be *firm, fair* and *honest.*

Reward them generously. And don't forget that *non-money rewards can often be far more effective.* Praise a salesman—when praise is due. Remember, it costs nothing! As a general rule, the carrot is more effective than the stick. Non-money rewards could take the form of straight praise, asking him to make a special presentation to the other salesmen, sending flowers to his wife (careful here!), giving him a special assignment, etc.

Now about *salary and incentives.* The first step is to decide the standard total earnings (including commission) of your average salesman. And don't be mean. Your conditions must be competitive. Otherwise you won't be able to hold your good men.

There is a lot of debate about how much commission salesmen should make. Norms vary from industry to industry. But the general consensus seems to be that 70 to 75 per cent of your average salesman's earnings should be straight salary. The rest should be variable earnings (commission, bonus, etc). This seems to represent a good balance between giving him some security and also some incentive to improve his performance.

Any incentive scheme you have should relate to objectives. The incentive scheme should make sense to the salesmen. Financial incentives should be linked to no more than *five* measurable performances objectives. Examples of measurable performance objectives would be: value of sales, value of salesman's contribution to overhead*, number of new accounts opened, percentage sales increase achieved on selected products, etc.

When you evaluate a salesman's performance, do so only against *his agreed objectives.* And talk about numbers—not about unmeasurables such as his 'attitude', etc.

Give him *feedback.* You like to know how you're doing. So do salesmen. Make sure they get as much data back from your accounts department as they need. They need to know how they're doing against their agreed objectives and compared to their colleagues.

---

* This is a particularly good one to use. Salesman's contribution to overhead = (sales revenue generated)–(direct costs)–(allocatable overheads per product)–(all expenses incurred by the salesman, including salary). It makes the salesman responsible for the real profitability of his area—and not just sales. He becomes in effect the 'general manager' for his area! He learns to push more profitable lines!

Let him in on the 'Big Picture'. If you want him to be part of your company team, then why not let him know how the company is doing? I know what you're thinking! But bear in mind that if you want your sales force to have a high morale, they must see that you trust them and respect them as colleagues in the enterprise. My advice is give them as much information as you can—even if it means taking a slight risk. You should also give them *a real voice in shaping your company policy.* Don't just impatiently listen to their complaints. Treat their comments and suggestions seriously. And when you get a useful suggestion, let them see you act on it! This is also a great tonic for morale.

'Stretch' each salesman occasionally. It's bad for a salesman to regard his job as routine. If you give him the occasional challenging assignment it can re-awaken his interest in the job. And you'll be surprised. Most people are capable of doing far better than the confines of their job might suggest. Examples of special assignments would be: to carry out some market research; make a special presentation to his colleagues; deputise for you in your absence; train a new salesman; etc.

Always be available. Salesmen are more highly motivated when they know their boss is *interested* and *approachable.* You should never be 'too busy' to listen to one of your salesmen who has a problem. In a way you become a sort of counsellor to your salesmen. The way to counsel effectively is:

(a) *Listen!*;
(b) No phone calls;
(c) Make sure there's plenty of time, so he doesn't feel rushed;
(d) Have a friendly, understanding attitude. This does not mean, of course, that you have to agree with him. But at least try to understand his point-of-view;
(e) Eventually, when the real problem comes out, *don't* solve it for the salesman. Help *him* solve it for himself!

Don't let your salesmen become too dependent on you. They're grown men. You should expect them to cope with their own problems.

Arrange frequent sales meetings (at least once a month). Very often sales meetings seem to consist merely of a list of complaints from the men. But that's no harm. Remember the loneliness and self-concept-damage they get on the job! They need to let off steam somewhere. They need to exchange experience with their colleagues.

You should arrange a purpose or theme for each meeting. But don't kid yourself. This is merely the 'window-dressing' for the real purpose. And the real purpose of a sales meeting is social. But it does pay off in terms of group morale and performance!

Help him identify with his products. You (I presume) are enthusiastic about your company's products. But then the company is your 'baby' after all. Your salesmen don't have quite the same personal stake in your business as you do. So you need to sell them often on their products. Sales meetings provide a good opportunity for this.

You are enthusiastic about your business. After all, it's your life. You should radiate this enthusiasm to your men. Let it show. Enthusiasm is catching!

Visit your salesmen in the field—and train them while you're at it. There's little point in trying to manage your salesmen by remote control. You should make a point of spending even half a day periodically with each man in the field.

Summary

Organising a high-performance sales force is not as simple as hiring a few men and letting them loose. You can't *make* them perform better. They are free adults. What you can do is *make* yourself become a better manager! It's far easier for you to change yourself than to change them!

You will notice that most of the tips have been aimed at getting the men 'switched on'. Motivation is the key—rather than elaborate sales control systems. And what you can do is behave in such a way that you create a climate in which *your salesmen will turn themselves on!*

If you haven't the time to do all these things and if your sales force is large enough (5 to 15 men) then perhaps you need a full-time sales manager!

CHAPTER ELEVEN

A DO-IT-YOURSELF ADVERTISING KIT

Advertising is one of the trickiest elements in your marketing-mix. Because (in most cases) no matter how much you spend on a particular campaign, you still don't know the extent to which any sales increase you may get is due to the advertising. Your sales may go up—or they may go down. What causes this? Maybe your advertising helps a lot. But you can't isolate its effect. In other words, the effect of your advertising gets lost somewhere in the effect of your total marketing-mix. The total mix produces your sales increase. And hopefully your advertising contributes to this mix. But even then it's usually impossible to put a number (or money) value on this contribution.

With direct selling you get direct feedback. And you can measure this feedback in terms of a calls/orders ratio. You don't get this direct feedback with advertising. And this is true even for very large companies who spend vast amounts advertising each of their products. There is only one exception to this. And that's what I call 'direct-response' advertising (e.g. some types of press advertisements which invite the reader to fill in a coupon and send money by post).

Now I'm not saying 'Don't advertise!' Advertising is valuable and worthwhile. All I'm trying to point out is that with advertising you're in a vague, unmeasurable area. Thus it is very, very risky.

Many businessmen seem to have a blind faith in the power of advertising. They feel that if you spend enough, then somehow your sales must increase. Nonsense! First of all, there is no proveable formula for how much you should spend.* Second, 'what

*Owner-managers often ask me for this formula. All I can say is that you do a balancing-act. You ask yourself two questions: (1) 'How much do I need to spend in order to get my intended message across to my target consumers?'; (2) 'How much can I afford to spend?' Then you strike a compromise figure!

you say' in your advertising and 'how you say it' is far more important than how much you spend!

> 'Half of the money I spent on advertising was wasted. The trouble is, I never knew which half!'

The above remark has been attributed to many sources, including Lord Leverhulme and Sam Wanamaker. It is one of those timeless phrases. And many advertising men still believe it's true today.

The Do-It-Yourself Advertising kit I'm presenting in this chapter will help you eliminate wastage in your advertising. Most advertising money gets wasted not in wrong choice of media (press, TV, etc) but because the *wrong message* is sent to the *wrong people.* This is where I hope my kit will help you. It focuses on the briefing process. This is what happens (or *should* happen) before any artist starts drawing pictures, etc. I have already persuaded a number of large British and Irish firms to use it successfully. So here's hoping it works for you, too. It's a simple method and (I hope you'll agree) effective.

But first a word about *advertising agencies.* As you probably know, agencies live on a commission system. The basic system is as follows: the agency buys advertising space or air-time for its clients at normal rates; then the media (newspaper, magazine or radio station) gives a refund of 15 per cent of the cost to the agency. This forms the agency's commission. Obviously the more the client spends, the juicier the commission!

If the client buys the advertising space himself (which he can do), he has to pay the full rates anyway. So in a sense, he might as well channel it through an agency. The agency supplies the client with its marketing, creative and media-buying expertise 'free'. Well, not exactly free – the 15 per cent commission more than covers the cost for the agency.

On top of this, if (as it always does) the agency incurs extra outside costs such as art-work, film production, story-board layouts, etc., it charges these costs to the client (+ 17.5 per cent commission to cover 'administrative expenses'!).

As you can see, agencies are mainly interested in big 'juicy' clients who spend a lot on advertising. So what can they do for you? You're probably not big and 'juicy'—yet! In your case you will probably find that the smaller agencies would be interested in your business—but only on a *straight fee* basis. What this means is that you would both agree on a straight fee of $x,000 which you would pay the agency each year. This would compensate them for the small media commission they would earn on your account. It would also enable them to give the same 'big client' attention to your account. But, of course, you have to pay. And even still, you have to compete for the agency executives' time against all their other clients.

It is worthwhile (if you haven't done so already) to have talks with a number of smaller agencies. See what they can offer you. And a word of warning! If you do decide to do business with one of them—make sure the contract is in writing—and make them stick to it.

It is not always a good idea for a small company to use an agency. If you apply yourself to it, you can often get a better job done yourself. Remember, generally the best advertising brains work on the biggest accounts. Small accounts often get the left-overs!

Remember, too, what the big client gets for his 15 per cent? He gets the agency's *marketing*, *media-buying* and *creative* talents. You can supply the *marketing* talent yourself. If you've worked properly with this book, believe me, you'll be better at it than most advertising executives. *Media-buying* is straightforward. You have a telephone. The salesman from any of the media will be on your doorstep within hours! You can buy *creative talent* directly. Most commercial artists who work in agencies also do extra private work after office hours. Get hold of one or two of these. Agency copywriters (the people who dream up the slogans, etc.) are also available after hours. If you have any flair for writing yourself, you can do the copywriting part. In this connection, I would recommend that you read a book called *The Art of Readable Writing* by Rudolf Flesch, published by Collier-Macmillan, London. It's a very good aid for writing copy which sells.

The Do-it-Yourself Kit in this chapter assumes that you are not using an agency. However, the same approach applies even if you are—because small clients need to do the strategic thinking for themselves anyway.

Stage one is mainly about helping you write a document, which advertising people call a 'copy strategy' or 'copy platform'. The one I'll tell you about, however, is different. It's a way of working out the two essential parts of a copy strategy. These are (a) the target audience, and (b) the message.

The copy strategy is *not* the advertising itself. It's what you should do *before* the advertising material itself is created. The copy strategy is in effect a 'briefing' or 'signpost'. If read by artists, copywriters and media-buyers in an agency, it would tell them what results are expected from the advertising—in *communication* terms. It would tell them what *message* is to be transmitted, and *to whom.* If you do use an agency, this document should be drawn up by your account executive in the agency plus yourself.

However, let's assume you have no agency. What this means then is that *you* are the media-buyer (and also perhaps the copywriter). You will probably hire part-time help for the 'art' side of it. So in effect, the copy strategy you write will be a briefing for yourself and your artist. (I know, it sounds crazy—but it works!).

The copy strategy is the *heart* of the advertising process. This is where most mistakes are made, and most money wasted. Essentially this document tells you *what* is expected from the advertising. It should *never* tell you *how* this is to be achieved.

There are two stages in the advertising process. There's first of all the *'What'* (i.e. the copy strategy). Then there's the *'How'* (i.e. after the 'What' is produced we must decide creatively *how* best to express it). The 'What' is *your* territory. The 'How' is the territory of artists and copywriters.

The best copy strategies are not too long. One or two pages is usually enough (otherwise it won't be read!). Although the document is short, it can take a long time to produce. It's a very creative activity!

What does it look like?

You divide the document, as follows, into five sections:

Stage 1. The copy strategy

(a) The Target Reader/Viewer/Listener

(b) Desired Impressions

(c) Limitations

(d) Deadline

(e) Evaluation Standards

We (or rather, you) will now have a go at drawing up a copy strategy. As you have already done the Marketing Do-it-Yourself Kit in chapters 4 and 5, this one should be fairly easy. Again I would ask you to stay with the original product you worked on in those two chapters. Refer back to the marketing-mix you planned in chapter 5—Exercise 8 (page 74). As part of your Communications-Mix you probably plan to advertise this product. (If not, then for this chapter, pick another one of your products which you normally *do* advertise.) So let's have a go then at the first two sections of the copy strategy in turn.

EXERCISE 11

The Target Reader/Viewer/Listener

You have already done this part! Just refer back to what you wrote down in chapter 4—Exercises 1, 2, 3 and 4.

All you do now is write a condensed description of your target customer below:

EXERCISE 12

Desired Impressions

This means the impression which you want your advertising to make on the target viewer's mind. In other words, the mental process you want to take place in his head (consciously or subconsciously) . . . which will lead to a purchase decision. It may be helpful to refer to the communications spectrum (see chapter 8):

Unawareness → awareness → comprehension → conviction → action.

Or better still, why not invent your own spectrum—one more appropriate to the state of your consumers? The length and complexity of the Desired Impressions will be influenced by how many stages of the above spectrum you wish to affect. You want to move your customer *from* where *to* where on the spectrum (with your advertising message)?

To get at the Desired Impressions, you must really project yourself into the target viewer's mind. Ask yourself the (often embarrassing) questions: 'Why on earth should he even bother to reach out and buy my product?'; 'Why should he even give it a thought?'.

Can you say something unique about your product, which none of your competitors is saying? Can you give your customers one good reason to think about your product? Can you give them a reason to buy? Could you create an attractive 'personality' or brand image for your product?

Now take it one step further . . . You *are* this person. Imagine the real situation where you are about to be confronted by an advertisement for the product in question. How are you feeling? Now imagine *you* are confronted with the actual ad.

It might be a 30-second TV impact or perhaps you are thumbing through a magazine. The impact is over. What traces should be left on your brain . . . which would lead to a purchase decision?

The best way to write down the Desired Impressions is to imagine the target viewer/reader talking to himself during the impact. Now try it . . . Remember you *are* this person! So talk to yourself as you would *realistically* like the target consumer to, in response to this impact.

Remember—what you are saying to yourself must (i) lead towards a purchase decision and (ii) be a realistic assessment of what is possible under the limitations of the circumstance (e.g. 30 seconds of fleeting attention).

Carrying out this type of exercise can be mind-bending for some executives. You need to practice it a few times before it becomes second nature.

Now, of course, your target viewer/reader won't actually talk to himself on this conscious level. But that doesn't matter. Because the 'self conversation' which you write down is a close facsimile of reality. While on a *conscious* level the consumer may only grunt or say 'Omo' to himself, he does have a 'conversation', subconsciously. In other words, each sensory message from your ad., is absorbed by the viewer's brain and incorporated into his own set of mental patterns.

This part of the copy strategy is the most difficult to do. Yet when finished, all you will have written are a couple of sentences within inverted commas.

So, have a go! You *are* your target customer. You are being confronted by an advertisement (for your product). What are you saying to yourself during the impact . . . ? (Remember what you say must move you along the spectrum).

"

____

____

____

____

____

____

____

"

____

It is obviously better if your Desired Impressions are different from your competitors'. However, it can happen in some highly competitive markets that the DI for your product is *similar* to your competitors'. In such cases, there is a special onus on the creative people to produce a really distinctive 'How'.

Limitations

This part is relatively easy. You write down all the elements which will impinge on the creative expression which follows your strategy. This would include the following, for example:

Total funds available (for media and production);

Corporate image requirements (e.g. the company logo must be featured, etc. . . .);

Media 'sacred cows' (e.g. if research has shown that press is more effective for this product, etc.).

Basically what you are doing here is telling the creative man beforehand about all the other restrictions within which he must work. Remember he prefers to know *before* he starts rather than after!

The golden rule here is not to overdo it. Only put down those restrictions which are strictly necessary. After all, you don't want to smother his creative scope completely. And above all, try *not* to trespass on his area of expertise. Remember you are not an artist! If you were, you wouldn't be using him!

Deadline

This speaks for itself. Creative people are notorious. They need to be chased.

Evaluation standards

All you are doing here is being fair. You are reminding the creative people and yourself about the name of the game. In this section, you simply state:

'The final creative proposals will be evaluated on two bases only –

(i) How well they meet this copy strategy (i.e. how well to communicate the Desired Impressions to the Target Viewer/Reader).
(ii) How well they meet the ten principles to help judge advertising.'

Ten principles to help judge advertising

You attach a copy of the 'ten principles' to your Copy Strategy. The ten principles are as follows: (just read them now—they make a lot of sense).

(1) Does the advertisement talk the customers' language?
(2) Does it concentrate on one selling idea?
(3) Does it concentrate on the most important and persuasive idea available?
(4) Does it present a unique and competitive idea?
(5) Does it involve the consumer?
(6) Is it credible and sincere?
(7) Is it simple, clear, complete?
(8) Does it clearly associate the selling idea with the brand name?
(9) Does it take full advantage of the medium?
(10) Does it move the customer along the communication spectrum?

Stage 2—Write the copy

When the copy strategy is complete, you have in effect a 'signpost' to direct the subsequent creative work. If you use an outside copywriter, just hand him the copy strategy and tell him to start writing!

If you write the copy yourself (and why not?) then you literally 'give yourself' the copy strategy. What you do then is 'change hats' and become a copywriter for an hour or two. Here are a few tips about copy writing:

(a) Keep the copy strategy before you all the time, as you write;

(b) Remember whom you're talking to—the *target reader.* Try to visualise him sitting in front of you. What would you say to him verbally? Then put it in writing!;

(c) Remember your objective—the *Desired Impressions.* Keep the DI in mind all the time, as you write.

(d) A word about your *style of writing.* Most people, when they write, go all 'formal and pompous' using long sentences and 'important' words. This is *not* good communication. The language which most people understand best is the language they learned as children. And that applies even to politicians and professors! It's also the type of language you use most naturally in everyday conversation.

The way you talk to a friend over a glass of beer—if you could put that in writing, it would be good copy. The formal style you might use if writing to a newspaper or another firm—that's bad copy!

If you don't believe me, just take a look through any book you enjoyed reading. You'll find that the author used a 'conversational' style. He writes as he speaks! So the rule is—use short, personal and conversational sentences. There are two examples of copy below. They both say the same thing. But one is easier to to read than the other. Guess which!

> 'This machine features the unique centrifugal de-compression system, which guarantees more consistent and predictable work-flow in the machine area and thus relieves the pressure at your loading bays.'

> 'You'll like our de-compression system. It makes the machine work at a steady rate. So relax! No more blockages in your loading bays!'

EXERCISE 13

Copywriting

You've got most of your copy strategy done already in Exercises 11 and 12. Get yourself a blank piece of paper. Have a go at writing your advertisement for a half-hour or so. You'll surprise yourself!

Stage 3—Brief the creative man

Let's assume he's a commercial artist, or a designer. All you do is hand him your copy-strategy plus copy. Also explain it to him verbally.

Then let him get on with the job. Never, never, never tell him *how* to do it! That's his area of professional expertise. If you try to tell him, you only switch him off. And you get mediocre results.

Stage 4—Evaluate the results

When you get back the designer's work, you simply say 'yes' or 'no'. But give reasons if you say 'no'. And these reasons should always be expressed in terms of not meeting the copy strategy or ten principles well enough. Creative people will accept this. Remember you don't want to switch them off!

Never judge advertising on aesthetic or design grounds. That's *not* your area of expertise—it's theirs. That is why they get paid.

So if you happen not to like a particular colour or illustration he uses—just keep quiet. Try to be objective and use only the copy strategy plus ten principles (plus, of course, your judgement) to evaluate.

If his work meets the brief, then please don't forget to give him plenty of praise. It costs nothing. But it really turns him on. Next time you give him a job, he'll really *work* on it. And that's what you want, isn't it?

Those are the four stages of the kit. The kit should also be used for other situations where you buy in creative expertise. It works for Public Relations as well as Product and Package design.

Before going on to chapter 12 (the last chapter!), please go back over this book again. Just skim through it at a leisurely pace, to refresh your memory.

CHAPTER TWELVE

MANAGE YOUR MARKETING SUCCESS

We started this book with the point that marketing is no more than business common-sense. A way of getting into the reality of marketing was used throughout the book–ISP (*I*nformation, *S*atisfying, *P*rofits). You have now worked at ISP in a very real sense.

I hope that, having used ISP once, you will now continue to practice it in your business. Each of your products needs ISP. So, why not put each of them in turn through this process (using the book as a memory-aid)?

And, once is not enough. Your customers (and their needs) are changing all the time. No product lasts forever. You have to be constantly on the look-out for new needs, new ideas and new products.

And what about exporting? There is no Divine Law which says that only big companies may export. In fact, some of the most successful small companies I know are very export-conscious. This is particularly important if you are producing speciality products in a small home market (e.g. Ireland). You have no choice. You *must* export. And there's nothing terribly strange about it. It's essentially the same ISP game—but played on a larger international stage.

Many owner-managers are put off by the idea of all the special shipping documents needed. Do remember that your national export promotion organisation is there to help you out on this with specialised assistance. Each country has its own export board. In Ireland, contact the Irish Export Board (Coras Trachtala). In Britain, the organisation is the Board of Trade. They also help with invaluable marketing advice and even sometimes with financial assistance. So think about it. Call in and have a talk with one of their advisers. Maybe he knows of a market opportunity which could be your salvation!

A very good way of building ISP into the routine of your business is to install *Marketing Plans.* This is what the more successful multinational companies do. You'll find it no problem—because *you've already written most of your first marketing plan!*

A marketing plan is a simple document. You write a separate one for each product. You divide it into four sections, as follows.

MARKETING PLAN

1. Background information
2. Marketing objectives for the coming year (*what* you intend to achieve)
3. Planned marketing mix (*How* you're going to get it)
4. Rationale behind objectives and marketing mix (*Why* you think that you'll achieve these objectives with this particular mix).

Quite apart from their being invaluable for sustaining the ISP approach, Marketing Plans are *very* useful when it comes to borrowing from your bank!

EXERCISE 14

Marketing Plan

This is the very last exercise (I promise!). But don't do it now. Wait until you have finished this chapter. Do it afterwards in your office. Start with the same product you've been working on already in this book. Then write a plan for each of your other products (or groups of products). Just read the brief explanations below, now. You can then refer back to them later.

Section 1–Background information. Here you put in the most important information you came up with in chapter 4 (part I of the Marketing Kit–the *I*nformation bit). You also include any historical market trend information (as per chapter 6). Any market research information should also be summarised here.

Section 2–Marketing objectives for the coming year (the 'what'). Here you put down your *planned* sales (as per chapter 6). Also–and this is important–write down your planned profitability with this product, in terms of *contribution to overhead.*

Section 3–Planned Marketing-Mix (the 'how'). You have the material for this in chapter 5 (part II of the marketing kit). Add in any additional material from chapter 7 (on *Price*), chapters 8, 9 and 10 on *Selling*, and chapter 11 on *Advertising.* Summarise your main decisions and write them down. You describe your planned mix–product mix, distribution mix* and communications mix.

Section 4–Rationale behind objectives and marketing mix (the 'why'). This is where you write down any supporting evidence

---

*You may have noticed that I did not deal specifically with the distribution mix in this book. The reason is that distribution systems vary so widely from one industry to another that there are few 'eternal truths' worth dealing with for the Owner-Manager.

you have. This could be material from the first section—or rather, your interpretation of some of that material.

This section is the most difficult. It's difficult because you can never *prove* what will happen in the future. But it is always worthwhile to look at what evidence you have, and 'formally' write down your interpretation of it. Show *why* you think your mix makes sense.

Why have Marketing Plans?

For much the same reasons that Unilever, Proctor & Gamble and General Motors have them!

(a) The sheer mental discipline of putting your thoughts in writing helps clarify your thinking.

(b) Plans help to manage your marketing better. Abraham Lincoln once said: 'If we could first know where we are, and whither we are tending to go, we could better judge what to do and how to do it'.

(c) It helps you monitor and control your progress. You check back every three months on each of your plans, and compare the planned objectives, with results actually achieved. You then may alter your mix slightly, or your objectives. But at least you know what's happening—and *you* are in control.

(d) As I said before, when you want to raise a loan, or look for financial support from government agencies or negotiate a business arrangement or merger, marketing plans are invaluable. *You* know what you're talking about. And *they* know that you are serious about your marketing.

(e) If you use an advertising or market research agency, Marketing Plans are essential in order to brief them properly.

Conclusion

As you have got this far with the book, I would like to thank you for staying with it. Don't forget to write those marketing plans. Do one for each product. And write in planned completion dates in your diary. You won't regret it. The success and growth of your business depends on your commitment to ISP.

One last thought—don't get *too* marketing-oriented! 'Product-fixation' can still be useful, as long as it doesn't blot out your vision of the market. It is also true to say: 'If you can't *make* it—don't sell it!'